SOUTH CAROLINA

DAILY DEVOTIONS FOR DIE-HARD FANS

GAMECOCKS

SOUTH CAROLINA

Daily Devotions for Die-Hard Fans: South Carolina Gamecocks
© 2010 Ed McMinn

Library of Congress Cataloging-in-Publication Data
13 ISBN Digit ISBN: 978-0-9801749-7-7

Manufactured in the United States of America.

Unless otherwise noted, scripture quotations are taken from the *Holy
Bible, New International Version*. Copyright © 1973, 1978, 1984, by the
International Bible Society. All rights reserved.

Go to http://www.die-hardfans.com for information about other titles in
the series.

Cover and interior design by Slynn McMinn.

Every effort has been made to identify copyright holders. Any
omissions are wholly unintentional. Extra Point Publishers should be
notified in writing immediately for full acknowledgement in future
editions.

GAMECOCKS

*To Kevin Long
and his son, Matthew,
a real team for God*

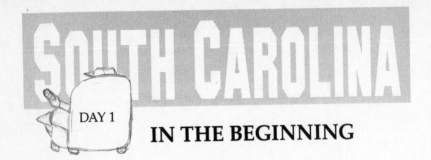

DAY 1

IN THE BEGINNING

Read Genesis 1, 2:1-3.

"God saw all that he had made, and it was very good" (v. 1:31).

Some students at tiny South Carolina College gave the state a Christmas present in 1892: a football team.

In October 1891, Furman University and Trinity College (now Duke) played an exhibition football game as part of State Fair Week at the fairgrounds in Columbia. The crowd included many of the 160 students at South Carolina College, who were so impressed that they set about forming a football team of their own.

The result was a Christmas Eve contest with Furman in 1892. The student body had voted on school colors and selected garnet and black, which hasn't changed, and a school mascot, the Jaguars, which has. The two played in Charleston as part of its holiday festivities.

The Carolina team was "hastily assembled for this one game, had no coach, very little practice, and played without faculty permission." In Furman, they were up against a squad that had been playing for four years.

"Christmas Eve dawned bright and cool, a perfect day for a football match." Special cars carried fans to Charleston's Base Ball Field for the game with kickoff at 3 p.m. Fans also were permitted to drive their carriages right up to the playing field. Some excited Charleston alumni provided carriages that transported players from both teams to the site.

Several hundred fans paid fifty cents each to watch the beginning of what was to be football at the University of South Carolina. As practically everyone expected, the experienced Furman team overwhelmed the game volunteers from Columbia 44-0. A student writer said "the boys boarded the train for Columbia slightly disfigured but still in the ring."

Beginnings are important, but what we make of them is even more important. Consider, for example, how far the South Carolina football program has come since that first game in 1892. Every morning, you get a gift from God: a new beginning. God hands to you as an expression of divine love a new day full of promise and the chance to right the wrongs in your life. You can use the day to pay a debt, start a new relationship, replace a burned-out light bulb, tell your family you love them, chase a dream, solve a nagging problem . . . or not.

God simply provides the gift. How you use it is up to you. People often talk wistfully about starting over or making a new beginning. God gives you the chance with the dawning of every new day.

You have the chance today to make things right – and that includes your relationship with God.

The most important key to achieving great success is to decide upon your goal and launch, get started, take action, move.
                                                            -- John Wooden

Every day is not just a dawn;
it is a precious chance to start over or begin anew.

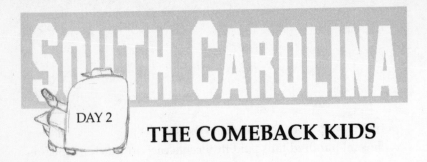

DAY 2

THE COMEBACK KIDS

Read Acts 9:1-22.

*"All those who heard him were astonished and asked,
'Isn't he the man who raised havoc in Jerusalem among
those who call on this name?'" (v. 21*

Against North Carolina in 1968, the Gamecocks pulled off what may well be the most remarkable comeback in South Carolina football history.

In his nine seasons as head coach in Columbia, Paul Dietzel's record was only 42-53-1. He owned the University of North Carolina, though. Against the Tar Heels, Dietzel was 5-0. His teams beat North Carolina 16-10 in 1967, 14-6 in 1969, 35-21 in 1970, and 31-23 in 1974. And then there is the incredible game of 1968.

For three quarters up in Chapel Hill, the Gamecocks did everything wrong. As a result, North Carolina led comfortably 27-3 headed into the final period. On the first play of the fourth quarter, Tommy Suggs hit Fred Zeigler with an 18-yard touchdown pass. The try for two on the conversion failed, but the Gamecocks were alive, trailing 27-9.

Momentum had clearly changed sides when the Heels fumbled the subsequent kickoff, the Gamecocks recovered, and two plays later fullback Warren Muir scored. This time Suggs ran it in for the two-point conversion; South Carolina trailed 27-17.

The defense forced a punt, and the offense drove 66 yards for another score, using up most of the quarter. Suggs threw to Rudy

Holloman for another two-point conversion, and South Carolina trailed only 27-25.

As North Carolina fans watched in horror and disbelief, the Heels fumbled at their own four after the kickoff. Suggs rolled to his right "and stepped four yards for the touchdown that decided a wild, wild ball game with just 4:54 left to play."

In a comeback for the ages, South Carolina scored 29 points in 10:01 and won 32-27.

Life will have its setbacks whether they result from personal failures or from forces and people beyond your control. Being a Christian and a faithful follower of Jesus Christ doesn't insulate you from getting into deep trouble. Maybe financial problems suffocated you. A serious illness put you on the sidelines. Or your family was hit with a great tragedy. Life is a series of victories and defeats. Winning isn't about avoiding defeat; it's about getting back up to compete again. It's about making a comeback of your own.

When you avail yourself of God's grace and God's power, your comeback is always greater than your setback. You are never too far behind, and it's never too late in life's game for Jesus to lead you to victory, to turn trouble into triumph. As it was with the Gamecocks against North Carolina in 1968 and with the apostle Paul, it's not how you start that counts; it's how you finish.

Turn a setback into a comeback.

-- Football coach Billy Brewer

**In life, victory is truly a matter of how you finish
and whether you finish with Jesus at your side.**

DAY 3

MIRACLE PLAY

Read Matthew 12:38-42.

"He answered, 'A wicked and adulterous generation asks for a miraculous sign!'" (v. 39)

uzzer-beaters are the salsa of college basketball, the highlight-film moments that remain long after the final score, or the final record, is forgotten," the miracle finishes that we remember. And South Carolina men's basketball has had more than its share.

On Jan. 7, 2001, Travis Kraft dropped a 25-foot, 3-point bomb on No. 5 Florida at the buzzer for a 69-68 win. (See Devotion No. 84.) "I can do it," he told Coach Eddie Fogler right before he did it.

On Feb. 1, 1998, No. 18 Cincinnati led USC 42-19 in the second half. With time running out, Antonio Grant launched a 25-foot prayer that was answered for a 67-65 miracle. "I've got knots on my forehead from people jumping all over me," Grant said.

On March 13, 1971, USC and North Carolina battled to the finish in the ACC Tournament title game. 6'3" guard Kevin Joyce controlled a jump ball against a 6'10" Tar Heel, tipping the ball to Tom Owens, who scored with one second left. "I don't even know if I touched the ball, but I think I got a piece of it," Joyce said about his miracle.

In 1972, Joyce was at it again, his 22-foot off-balance jumper with one second left beating Temple for the Gamecocks' first-ever NCAA Tournament win. In the 1968 debut of Carolina Coliseum with time running out, John Roche, still considered USC's greatest player ever, nailed a jump shot to beat Auburn 51-49. In 1974, Brian Winters hit from 16 feet with two seconds left to beat No. 6 Marquette 60-58. Frank McGuire said of the win, "I've had none finer." In 1994, Emmett Hall scored with three seconds left after a pass from guard Carey Rich to stun Kentucky 75-74.

Miracle finishes all.

Miracles defy rational explanation – like last second, game-winning shots from 25 feet. Escaping with minor abrasions from an accident that totals your car. Or recovering from an illness that seemed terminal. Underlying the notion of miracles is that they are rare instances of direct divine intervention that reveal God.

But life shows us quite the contrary, that miracles are anything but rare. Since God made the world and everything in it, everything around you is miraculous. Even you are a miracle. Your life can be mundane, dull, and ordinary, or it can be spent in a glorious attitude of childlike wonder and awe. It depends on whether or not you see the world through the eyes of faith; only through faith can you discern the hand of God in any event. Only through faith can you see the miraculous and thus see God.

Jesus knew that miracles don't produce faith, but rather faith produces miracles.

Do you believe in miracles? Yes!
– Broadcaster Al Michaels when U.S. defeated USSR in hockey in 1980
Winter Games

**Miracles are all around us, but it takes
the eyes of faith to see them.**

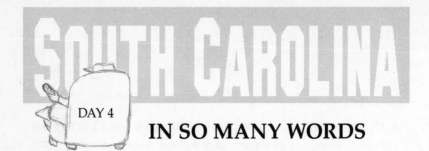

SOUTH CAROLINA

DAY 4

IN SO MANY WORDS

Read Matthew 12:33-37.

"For out of the overflow of the heart the mouth speaks. The good man brings good things out of the good stored up in him, and the evil man brings evil things out of the evil stored up in him" (vv. 34b-35).

The Gamecocks were behind against a team they'd never beaten, but quarterback Phil Petty had some words for his teammates. They listened and they won.

Under Coach Lou Holtz, Petty quarterbacked South Carolina to the best two-year run in school history: 8-4 in 2000 and 9-3 in 2001, both seasons ending with wins over Ohio State in the Outback Bowl.

On Sept. 29, 2001, the Gamecocks, 4-0 and ranked 15th, hosted Alabama and did as they'd always done against the Crimson Tide: They fell behind, trailing 36-24 with nine minutes left. But Petty knew the offense had been moving all day. "It was just a game of frustration," he said. "We were close on some things but didn't convert." So Petty got his guys together on the sideline and told them what they had to do to win. The gist of his message was "Just do your job." "If we could go out there and execute our jobs," Petty said, "we'd do well enough to win the game."

The guys listened, and Carolina scored. When the defense held, Petty knew he could find a hole in the Tide defense and "go down and score." The Gamecocks moved to the seven where Petty saw

Rodney Trafford was one-on-one with his defender. "The guy had inside leverage on him," Petty said. "So he did the old basketball fake inside and came outside, and when he did, I threw it on time and converted the touchdown."

The Gamecock offensive players had listened to their quarterback's words, done what he said, and rallied with two late touchdowns for a milestone 37-36 win.

These days, everybody's got something to say and likely as not a place to say it. Talk radio, 24-hour sports and news TV channels, *The View*. Talk has really become cheap, and much of it's not as helpful as Phil Petty's words were.

But words still have power, and that includes not just those of the talking heads, hucksters, and pundits on television, but ours also. Our words are perhaps the most powerful force we possess for good or for bad. The words we speak today can belittle, wound, humiliate, and destroy. They can also inspire, heal, protect, and create. Our words both shape and define us. They also reveal to the world the depth of our faith.

We should never make the mistake of underestimating the power of the spoken word. After all, speaking the Word was the only means Jesus had to get his message across – and look what he managed to do.

We must always watch what we say, because others sure will.

Never let your mouth write a check that your body can't cash.
– Lou Holtz

Choose your words carefully; they are the most powerful force you have for good or for bad.

DAY 5

THE PRIZE

Read Philippians 3:10-16.

*"I press on toward the goal to win the prize for which God
has called me heavenward in Christ Jesus" (v. 14).*

Where's the trophy?" Somebody must have asked that question
as the Gamecocks flew home from the 2006 Liberty Bowl. One
thing for sure: It wasn't on the plane.

On Dec. 29, 2006, South Carolina defeated Houston 44-36 in the
Liberty Bowl in Memphis. The championship trophy – a replica
of the Liberty Bell in Philadelphia -- didn't make it aboard the
return flight to Columbia. Instead, it wound up in the hands of
long snapper Scott Morgan, who missed the flight.

The saga of the Liberty Bowl trophy began after the game
when the team bus returned to the hotel in downtown Memphis
where the Gamecocks were staying. A disembarked graduate
assistant tapped on the glass and asked Morgan to grab the trophy.
Morgan obliged and left the trophy in his hotel room as he and
his teammates enjoyed a night on the town. He overslept the next
morning, waking two hours late with the "sinking feeling he
was alone in Memphis – sort of. 'I know they're not here. I know
they've left,' Morgan recalled thinking. 'I roll over and the Liberty
Bowl trophy is still sitting on my floor. I was like 'Oh, great.'"

Morgan fortunately hooked up with his roommates, and four
guys and the 80-pound trophy all crammed into a Pontiac sedan.
After nearly 600 miles on the road, the "traveling trophy and its

handlers rolled into Columbia" before daylight Sunday morning. The trophy spent the night on a coffee table before it was handed over – none the worse for wear – to the equipment manager. "We should be grateful that Scott is relatively responsible," said a relieved director of football operations.

Even the most modest and self-effacing among us can't help but be pleased by prizes, honors, trophies, certificates, and plaques. They symbolize the approval and appreciation of others, whether it's an All-American team, an Employee of the Month trophy, a plaque for sales achievement, or the sign declaring yours as the neighborhood's prettiest yard.

Such prizes and awards are often the culmination of the pursuit of personal achievement and accomplishment. They represent accolades and recognition from the world. Nothing is inherently wrong with any of that as long as we keep them in perspective.

That is, we must never let such awards become idols that we worship or lower our sight from the greatest prize of all and the only one truly worth winning. It's one that won't rust, collect dust, or leave us wondering why we worked so hard to win it in the first place. The ultimate prize is eternal life, and it's ours through Jesus Christ.

A gold medal is a wonderful thing, but if you're not enough without it, you'll never be enough with it.
-- *John Candy in* Cool Running

The greatest prize of all doesn't require competition to claim it; God has it ready to hand to you through Jesus Christ.

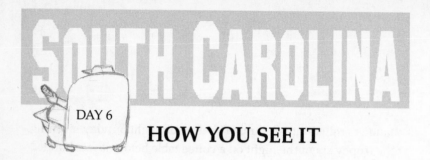

DAY 6

HOW YOU SEE IT

Read John 20:11-18.

"Mary stood outside the tomb crying" (v. 11).

It's a matter of perspective. Mark Berson is the best men's soccer coach South Carolina has ever had. Mark Berson is the worst men's soccer coach South Carolina has ever had.

Those are the differing perspectives Berson sometimes has about himself when he looks in the mirror in the morning. Actually, they're both true because through the 2010 season, Berson is the only men's soccer coach South Carolina has ever had. "At least I know I'm right both times," he once said about his perspectives.

Berson launched one of the nation's consistently most successful programs more than three decades ago without a stadium, a single uniform, a schedule, or any equipment. He really didn't have a conception of what the program could really be.

So here's what it is: As the 2010 season began, Berson's USC teams had won 417 matches, which ranks him second among the nation's active soccer college coaches. Eighteen Gamecock teams have appeared in the NCAA Tournament with the 1993 squad making it to the finals.

Hired in 1978 by USC Athletics Director Jim Carlen, Berson was in charge of every detail. He "recruited the players, scheduled games, drove the team bus, washed uniforms, lined the field and slept many nights in his office." When his first bleachers showed up at what is now Stone Stadium, Berson and his team unloaded

COCKS

am often practiced at one end of a
at a cemetery on the other end.
evity, though, didn't keep Berson
uring a five-game losing streak in
lf the worst soccer coach in USC
nged when the team lost only one
son. As one writer put it, Berson "is
atus."
g way toward determining whether
despair, anger, and hopelessness or
ith joy and hope. Mary is a good
morning, she stood by Jesus' tomb
crying, her heart broken, because she still viewed everything
through the perspective of Jesus' death. But how her attitude, her
heart, and her life changed when she saw the morning through
the perspective of Jesus' resurrection.

So it is with life and death for all of us. You can't avoid death, but
you can determine how you perceive it. Is it fearful, dark, fraught
with peril and uncertainty? Or is it a simple little passageway to
glory, the light, and loved ones, an elevator ride to paradise?

It's a matter of perspective that depends totally on whether or
not you're standing by Jesus' side when it arrives.

*For some people it's the end of the rainbow, but for us it's the end of the
finish line.*

— *Rower Larisa Healy*

**Whether death is your worst enemy
or a solicitous chauffeur is a matter of perspective.**

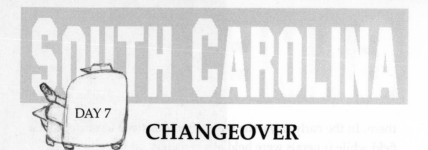
DAY 7

CHANGEOVER

Read Romans 6:1-14.

"Just as Christ was raised from the dead through the glory of the Father, we too may live a new life" (v. 4).

You're gonna remove the "Beat Clemson" signs from Williams-Brice Stadium? That's right. How the times they did change when Steve Spurrier hit town.

Spurrier became South Carolina's 32nd head coach on Nov. 23, 2004. As sportswriter Ron Morris put it, "Plain and simple, Spurrier inherited a mess. He took over a program sorely lacking in discipline and virtually void of direction." Spurrier immediately set about making changes.

He dismissed about a dozen players from the team for various transgressions. He changed players' diets from an emphasis on fried chicken and dessert to fruit, vegetables, and grilled chicken. He declared that if the players didn't want to work hard enough, he'd pay their cab fare to another school.

He changed what the players expected of themselves. "When coach Spurrier came in he had high expectations," said senior offensive lineman Na'Shan Goddard, who went on to a pro career. "Before it was just play tough, play tough, and that's what we were doing. We would lose and teams (would) be like, 'Y'all are tough.'" Just being tough wasn't good enough anymore.

The change Spurrier made that raised the most eyebrows among the Gamecock faithful was asserting that both the players and the fans put too much importance on beating Clemson. This resulted from Spurrier's insistence that the Gamecocks set the winning of championships among their team goals. The key games thus became those against the perennial conference and division powers: Tennessee, Florida, and Georgia. As part of the shift in emphasis, the "Beat Clemson" signs came down.

"An overhaul was needed," Morris wrote when Steve Spurrier arrived. That meant changes, and the old ball coach made them.

Anyone who asserts no change is needed in his or her life isn't paying attention. Every life has doubt, worry, fear, failure, frustration, unfulfilled dreams, and unsuccessful relationships in some combination. The memory and consequences of our past often haunt and trouble us.

Recognizing the need for change in our lives, though, doesn't mean the changes that will bring about hope, joy, peace, and fulfillment will occur. We need some power greater than ourselves or we wouldn't be where we are.

So where can we turn to? Where lies the hope for a changed life? It lies in an encounter with him who is the Lord of all Hope: Jesus Christ. For a life turned over to Jesus, change is inevitable. With Jesus in charge, the old self with its painful and destructive ways of thinking, feeling, loving, and living is transformed.

A changed life is always only a talk with Jesus away.

I believe in the power of sport and play to change lives.
-- Olympic gold medalist Catriona Le May Doan

In Jesus lie the hope and the power
that change lives.

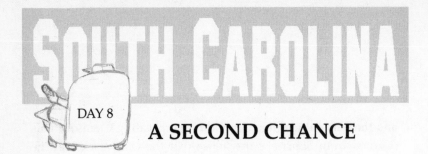
DAY 8

A SECOND CHANCE

Read John 7:53-8:11.

"'Then neither do I condemn you,' Jesus declared. 'Go now and leave your life of sin'" (v. 8:11).

Rarely in football does a team get a second chance in a game. Against Clemson in 1984, the Gamecocks got two.

The 1984 season is the most successful in school history. It included wins over Georgia and Notre Dame and a nationally televised victory over FSU. In the season finale, though, the 9-1 Gamecocks appeared to be still feeling the effects of the upset loss the week before to Navy that had foiled their chances of a national championship as they fell behind the Tigers 21-3 late in the second quarter. With 46 seconds left in the half, they got their first mulligan. A field goal was missed, but Clemson was offsides. With the ball moved to the five, Coach Joe Morrison decided to go for the touchdown. Quinton Lewis scored, and the Gamecocks had cut the margin to 21-10 at halftime.

In the third quarter, Tony Guyton and Willie McIntee combined to sack the Clemson quarterback for a safety to make it 21-12 as the last quarter began. Scott Hagler's 41-yard field goal cut the lead to 21-15.

A punt backed Carolina up to its 14 with only 3:07 left. Field general Mike Hold led the team on one of the most memorable drives in school history and scored from the one on a quarterback keeper with only 54 seconds left. With the score tied at 21, a Carolina win seemed a cinch. After all, Hagler's last extra point had tied the school record of 42 straight.

But it took a second second chance for the Gamecocks to win. Incredibly, Hagler missed the kick, but perhaps even more incredibly, Clemson had twelve men on the field. Given a second chance a second time in the game, Hagler was true.

Thanks in great part to the two second chances that meant an eight-point swing, South Carolina had a 22-21 win.

"If I just had a second chance, I know I could make it work out." Ever said that? If only you could go back and tell your dad one last time you love him, take that job you passed up rather than relocate, or go out on that date you turned down. If only you had a second chance.

As the story of Jesus' encounter with the adulterous woman illustrates, with God you always get a second chance. No matter how many mistakes you make, God will never give up on you. Nothing you can do puts you beyond God's saving power. You always have a second chance because with God your future is not determined by your past or who you used to be. It is determined by your relationship with God through Jesus Christ.

God is ready and willing to give you a second chance – or a third chance or a fourth chance – if you will give him a chance.

I have to thank God for giving me the gift that he did as well as a second chance for a better life.
-- Olympic figure skating champion Oksana Baiul

**You get a second chance with God
if you give him a chance.**

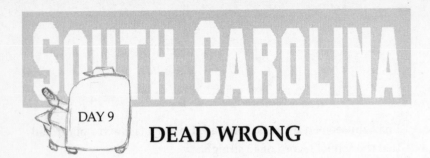

DAY 9

DEAD WRONG

Read Matthew 26:14-16; 27:1-10.

"When Judas, who had betrayed him, saw that Jesus was condemned, he was seized with remorse" (v. 27:3).

Football coach Jim Carlen was dead wrong when he said one of his football players wouldn't make a good baseball player.

Randy Martz had all the makings of a superb drop-back quarterback when he came to South Carolina from Elizabethton, Penn., in 1975. He was also a pretty good pitcher though he wasn't drafted by the pros out of high school.

Martz' career in Columbia was doomed, however, when Carlen switched from a pro-style offense to the veer, which required a mobile, running quarterback, which Martz wasn't. So he never lettered, spending his time on the scout squad running the opposition's plays for the defense to practice against.

Carlen didn't allow his quarterbacks to play baseball, so Martz had no chance to give baseball a shot. Before the 1977 baseball season began, however, Carlen told Gamecock baseball coach June Raines, "If you want that Martz boy, you can have him, but he won't help you because he's no athlete."

Carlen was about as dead wrong as a coach could ever be.

Martz started 16 games for the Gamecocks that spring. He compiled a 14-0 record, a 1.98 ERA, and pitched South Carolina to within one win of the NCAA championship at the College World Series. He was named to every All-America team and won the

Lefty Gomez Award as the nation's best amateur baseball player. In both of his no-decisions, Martz left with the lead.

After that one sensational season, the Chicago Cubs made him their first-round draft choice. In three seasons in the majors with the Cubs and the White Sox, Martz won 17 games -- including 11 in 1982 -- before an arm injury ended his career. Not bad for a player a coach said was no athlete.

There's wrong, there's dead wrong, and there's Judas wrong. We've all been wrong in our lives, but we can at least honestly ease our conscience by telling ourselves we'll never be as wrong as Judas was. A close examination of Judas' actions, however, reveals that we can indeed replicate in our own lives the mistake Judas made that drove him to suicidal despair.

Judas ultimately regretted his betrayal of our Lord, but his sorrow and remorse, however boundless, could not save him. His attempt to undo his initial wrong was futile because he tried to fix everything himself rather than turning to God in repentance and begging for mercy.

While we can't literally betray Jesus to his enemies as Judas did, we can match Judas' failure in our own lives by not turning to God in Jesus' name and asking for forgiveness for our sins. In that case, we ultimately will be as dead wrong as Judas was.

Don't practice until you get it right. Practice until you can't get it wrong.

-- Source unknown

A sin is the first wrong; failing to ask God for forgiveness of it is the second.

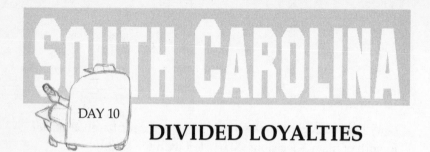

DAY 10

DIVIDED LOYALTIES

Read Matthew 6:1-24.

"No one can serve two masters" (v. 24a).

Divided loyalties happen in the best of families; some cheer for South Carolina; some cheer for Clemson. Perhaps nobody else in history, though, can match the sundered loyalties Cary Cox encountered. He was a team captain for both the Tigers and the Gamecocks.

Probably nothing short of the upheaval engendered by World War II could produce Cox's unique situation. He played for Clemson in 1942. When he signed for the Navy's V-12 program, he was promptly called up and assigned to USC for training. He was also ordered to report for football practice.

Cox was named a Gamecock team captain, which was fine until the week of Big Thursday when he had some qualms about playing against his old teammates. When he explained his moral dilemma to his commander, he was told, "Cox, I can't promise you'll get your commission if you play Thursday, but I can promise you that you won't get it if you don't play." "It's amazing what a little counseling can do to assuage a troubled conscience," Cox said. Still, he felt bad about the situation and called Coach Frank Howard at Clemson, who told him to "go out there and play [his] heart out."

South Carolina won easily 33-6. One play included a line shift that made Cox, the center, an eligible receiver. He caught a 28-yard pass, and as he was disentangling himself from the pile, someone kicked him in his backside. It was Coach Howard, who told him, "Son, I told you to play your heart out, but I didn't say nothing about catching no passes."

Cox completed the war as a captain and returned to Clemson in 1946. He became a legend in state football when he was captain of the 1947 Tigers.

Clemson or South Carolina: In 1943, Cary Cox had to decide where his loyalty lay. You probably understand the stress that comes with divided loyalties. The Christian work ethic drives you to be successful. The world, however, often makes demands and presents images that conflict with your devotion to God: movies deride God; couples play musical beds in TV sitcoms; and TV dramas portray Christians as killers following God's orders.

It's Sunday morning and the office will be quiet or the golf course won't be crowded. What do you do when your heart and loyalties are pulled in two directions? Jesus knew of the struggle we face; that's why he spoke of not being able to serve "two masters," that we wind up serving one and despising the other. Put in terms of either serving God or despising God, the choice is stark and clear.

Your loyalty is to God -- always.

I am the most loyal player money can buy.
> *-- Former major leaguer Don Sutton*

**God does not condemn you for being successful
and enjoying popular culture, but your loyalty
must lie first and foremost with him.**

DAY 11

THE PANIC BUTTON

Read Mark 4:35-41.

"He said to his disciples, 'Why are you so afraid? Do you still have no faith?'" (v. 40)

It was a good time for the Gamecocks to panic. Clock running out. No time outs. Fourth down at the Georgia one. But they didn't panic, and the result was Brandon Bennett over the top.

In Athens on Sept. 23, 1993, Georgia and South Carolina played one of the most exciting games in the annals of the long rivalry. Georgia led 21-17 in the fourth quarter when Gamecock sophomore quarterback Steve Taneyhill told his huddled teammates to relax, not to panic. "We're going to go down there and we're going to score," he said.

South Carolina did just that. As the clock wound down and with no time outs left, Taneyhill hit tight end Boomer Foster for a first down at the Georgia two. Two straight line smashes failed to score. "We don't have much time," Taneyhill told his teammates as they huddled for the last time. "Everybody said, all right, we got it, we got it," Bennett remembered. But they didn't. Bennett tried to go over the top but the defense yanked him back.

Now the clock was rolling down its last few seconds with the Gamecocks facing fourth and one. With no time to huddle, Taneyhill didn't even try to disguise the play. "Same play!" he screamed as the offense lined up. With apparent calm and no panic, Taneyhill "went through the cadence. It was blocked perfectly." Bennett went over the top again, and "they kind of stopped me a little, but then I flipped over to make sure I got in there."

With two seconds to spare, South Carolina scored and won 23-21.

Have you ever experienced that suffocating sensation of fear escalating into full-blown panic? Maybe the time when you couldn't find your child at the mall or at the beach? Or the heart-stopping moment when you looked out and saw that tornado headed your way?

As the disciples illustrate, the problem with panic is that it debilitates us. Here they were, professional fishermen in the bunch, and they let a bad storm panic them into helplessness. All they could do was wake up an exhausted Jesus.

We shouldn't be too hard on them, though, because we often make the same mistake they did when we encounter a situation fraught with danger and fear. That is, we underestimate both Jesus' power and his ability to handle our crises.

We have a choice when fear clutches us: We can assume Jesus no longer cares for us, surrender to it, and descend into panic, or we can remember how much Jesus loves us and resist fear and panic by trusting in him.

Look at misfortune the same way you look at success. Don't Panic. Do your best and forget the consequences.
-- Former major league manager Walt Alston

To plunge into panic is to believe
– quite wrongly -- that Jesus is incapable
of handling the crises in our lives.

DAY 12

ONE TOUGH COOKIE

Read 2 Corinthians 11:21b-29.

"Besides everything else, I face daily the pressure of my concern for all the churches" (v. 28).

This league is a bloodbath. That's what makes it so great."

So spoke one of South Carolina's greatest – and toughest – basketball players. He was John Roche, a "snarling alley guy the East Side [of New York was] proud to call its own." And so were Gamecock fans. When Roche returned to Columbia in 2007 for a celebration of 100 years of South Carolina basketball, Coach Dave Odom called him "the most revered name in Gamecock basketball history."

Roche was the ACC Player of the Year in both 1969 and 1970, the first player in league history to receive the honor his first two years. He was the runner-up in 1971 and went on to an eight-year professional career. His #11 jersey was retired in 1971, and he was inducted into the USC Hall of Fame in 1979.

Roche was a star ball handler with a textbook jump shot, but he made his reputation with his legendary toughness as much as his talent, living up to the reputation that preceded him from the streets of New York City. In 1970 in the semifinal game of the ACC Tournament against Wake Forest, he tore ligaments in his left ankle. He came to the gym the next night on crutches, but set them aside and played.

Roche's teammate, John Ribbock, was so ferocious Roche and

GAMECOCKS

his fellow New Yorker, Tom Owens, nicknamed him "Instant Savage." Nevertheless, the team considered Roche the toughest of the bunch. "He goes crazy sometimes," Owens said. "He's so intense, he wants to win so badly. He has that look, like he's asking for trouble – an amazing hothead. Ask him."

John Roche was one tough cookie.

You don't have to be a legendary South Carolina basketball player to be tough. In America today, toughness isn't restricted to physical accomplishments and brute strength. Going to work every morning even when you feel bad, sticking by your rules for your children in a society that ridicules parental authority, making hard decisions about your aging parents' care often over their objections — you've got to be tough every day just to live honorably, decently, and justly.

Living faithfully requires toughness, too, though in America chances are you won't be imprisoned, stoned, or flogged this week for your faith as Paul was. Still, contemporary society exerts subtle, psychological, daily pressures on you to turn your back on your faith and your values. Popular culture promotes promiscuity, atheism, and gutter language; your children's schools have kicked God out; the corporate culture advocates amorality before the shrine of the almighty dollar.

You have to hang tough to keep the faith.

Winning isn't imperative, but getting tougher in the fourth quarter is.
– Bear Bryant

**Life demands more than mere physical toughness;
you must be spiritually tough too.**

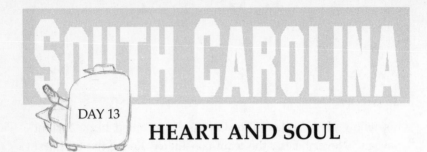

DAY 13

HEART AND SOUL

Read Romans 12:1-2.

*"Therefore, I urge you, brothers, in view of God's mercy,
to offer your bodies as living sacrifices, holy and pleasing
to God – this is your spiritual act of worship" (v. 1).*

Until she discovered a newfound commitment, one of the world's greatest runners was ready to quit.

In 2006, Natasha Hastings was ready to chuck it all. Injuries had virtually wiped out her sophomore year at USC. "It had just gotten to a point where I felt I had been through so much injury-wise," she said. "I was in a (protective) boot for two months. I couldn't do anything. . . . For a while it wasn't fun anymore." She gained weight during the inactivity forced by the injuries, which varied from tendonitis in her ankle to a respiratory infection.

During the offseason, though, Hastings decided she shouldn't throw away the talent she had inherited from her parents, especially her mother, herself a great runner. "I just realized God was putting me through some things," Hastings said. She responded with a renewed commitment to running that included changing her diet to shed the extra weight, early-morning workouts, and driving from her home in Atlanta to Columbia three times each week to train during the winter break.

The result was a string of achievements that now has Hastings considered among the world's greatest runners. In 2007, she won both the SEC and the NCAA championships in the 400m, setting a new record in the latter. The wins kept piling up both individually and as part of South Carolina's 4X400 relay team. The collegiate track coaches named her the national Women's Track Athlete of the Year.

The results of her commitment culminated in a Gold Medal in the 4X400 relay in the 2008 Summer Olympics in Beijing.

When you stood in a church and recited your wedding vows, did you make a decision that you could walk away from when things got tough or did you make a lifelong commitment? Is your job just a way to get a paycheck, or are you committed to it?

Commitment almost seems a dirty word in our society these days, a synonym for chains, an antonym for freedom. Perhaps this is why so many people are afraid of Jesus: Jesus demands commitment. To speak of offering yourself as "a living sacrifice" is not to speak blithely of making a decision but of heart-body-mind-and-soul commitment.

But commitment actually means "purpose and meaning," especially when you're talking about your life. Commitment makes life worthwhile. Anyway, in insisting upon commitment, Jesus isn't asking anything from you that he hasn't already given to you himself. His commitment to you was so deep that he died for you.

Talent takes you to a place, but commitment takes you to the finish line.
-- USC track and field coach Curtis Frye

Rather than constraining you,
commitment to Jesus lends meaning to your life,
releasing you to move forward with purpose.

DAY 14

DECIDE FOR YOURSELF

Read John 6:60-69.

"The words I have spoken to you are spirit and they are life. Yet there are some of you who do not believe" (vv. 63b-64a).

The Gamecock football team once made a decision that killed a bowl game.

The South Carolina squad of 1945 finished with an unusual 2-3-3 record. The team was also unusual in that it got better as the season went on but not because of more practice and more experience. The team improved as young men were discharged from the service and came home. For example, halfback Bobby Giles joined the team in mid-season.

On Thanksgiving Day the Gamecocks met Wake Forest, which, said one sportswriter, "was of little interest to anyone except fans of the two colleges." At the time, that probably was true. The Deacons were favored, but South Carolina got an eight-yard touchdown pass from Bill Carr to Lyle Hanson and a brilliant run from halfback Charles Brembs, who turned a short pass from Dan Haralson into a 43-yard score. The game ended in a 13-13 tie.

Meanwhile, in Jacksonville, Fla., the Lions Club decided to host a bowl game. A similar situation was perking in Columbia with the announcement of the establishment of the Tobacco Bowl with the Gamecocks as the host team in a rematch of the Wake Forest game.

GAMECOCKS

A formal invitation was delayed, however, as plans for the bowl were formulated. A week after plans for the Columbia game were announced, the Gamecock players decided to accept an invitation from that brand new Gator Bowl in Jacksonville. The next day officials in Columbia cancelled plans for the Tobacco Bowl and never revived it.

The decisions you made along the way shaped your life at every pivotal moment. Some decisions you made suddenly and frivolously; some you made carefully and deliberately; some were forced upon you. Perhaps decisions made for frivolous reasons have determined how your life unfolds, and you may have discovered that some of those spur-of-the-moment decisions have turned out better than your carefully considered ones.

Of all your life's decisions, however, none is more important than one you cannot ignore: What have you done with Jesus? Even in his time, people chose to follow Jesus or to reject him, and nothing has changed; the decision must still be made and nobody can make it for you. Ignoring Jesus won't work either; that is, in fact, a decision, and neither he nor the consequences of your decision will go away. Carefully considered or spontaneous – how you arrive at a decision for Jesus doesn't matter; all that matters is that you get there.

If you make a decision that you think is the proper one at the time, then that's the correct decision.

-- John Wooden

A decision for Jesus may be spontaneous or considered; what counts is that you make it.

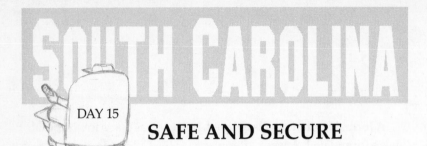

DAY 15

SAFE AND SECURE

Read Psalm 112.

"[A righteous man's] heart is secure, he will have no fear"
(v. 8a).

Carolina Fieldhouse was well fortified with its usual contingent of security personnel and local police, but they couldn't keep one player's mama and her purse off the court during a fight.

In early February 1961, the Gamecock freshmen whipped Wake Forest's rookies 99-83. Near the end of the game, a brawl broke out, and that's when Ronnie Collins' mama injected herself into the game. Collins, who would earn first team All-ACC honors as a senior in 1964, was the star of that team, and he always insisted he was not part of the brouhaha, which escalated until game officials struggled to restore order. Right in the middle of all those pushing and shoving players, a woman walked onto the court. She was wearing a long overcoat and a purse with which she could fend off any Wake Forest player who even thought of approaching her. The woman was Carrie Collins.

"I was scared Ronnie was going to get hurt," she later explained. "Darn, what's she doing out here?" was Ronnie's reaction as he stood next to a police officer and watched her approach. "I didn't fight. I might have swung my purse," Mrs. Collins said. "I might have scared them to death with that purse."

Collins remembered that a police office escorted his mother back to her seat, telling her, "You need to behave yourself, Mrs.

Collins."

Since fights were quite common in the ACC in those days, the fieldhouse was built with a rail to keep people off the court. That didn't even slow Mrs. Collins down. "I jumped the rail and I went out there on the court," she recalled. "They had a big laugh about that. I went out there to see if Ronnie was all right."

Her son was quite safe and secure except for the inevitable ribbing that followed from his teammates. He was forever known at USC as a momma's boy.

Home burglar alarms. Keyless systems that let us avoid fumbling for our vehicle keys at night. Cell phones so we can know where our children are. Passwords for our computers.

Such security measures are all responses to the basic fact that the world is an unsafe place. But if a thug is determined to do us harm, he will despite all our precautions. We know that, so anxiety and angst are a subliminal part of our lives, right?

Not necessarily. Those who love the Lord have a confidence and a sense of security that have nothing to do with punch pads and mace. To walk in the fear of God is to live in faith and courage; it is to live securely without worry and anxiety even in the midst of trouble. Our security lies in our faith, and our faith is in the eternal and the divine, not the temporary and the secular.

One thing I refuse to do is live in fear.
-- American swimmer Erik Vendt on the danger of terrorism
at the 2004 Olympics

Our faith provides for eternal security even among the perils of everyday life.

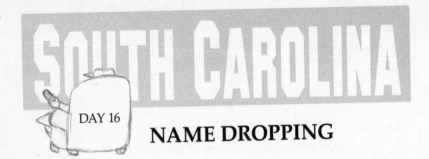

DAY 16

NAME DROPPING

Read Exodus 3:13-20.

*"God said to Moses, 'I AM WHO I AM. This is what
you are to say to the Israelites: 'I AM has sent me to you'"*
(v. 14).

Fire Ants and Black Magic. Boo. The Pullets. Many of South Carolina's athletes and coaches have had some rather interesting and novel nicknames over the years.

"Fire Ants and Black Magic" refers to the 1984 Gamecock football team, still the most successful in school history. Defensive coordinator Tom Gadd applied the fire-ant nickname to the defense while he was grading film, declaring they "looked like a bunch of fire ants getting after the football." Gamecock head coach Joe Morrison (1983-88) was known as "Old Dependable" from his fourteen seasons in pro football with the New York Giants.

W.H. "Dixie" Whaley was USC's first paid football coach. "Boo" is the nickname of the most celebrated athlete in Gamecock football history: George Rogers.

Fans slapped "The Catch" to Robert Brooks' sensational one-handed, over-the-shoulder 36-yard reception for a touchdown in 1988's 23-10 win over Georgia. When women's basketball first began at USC, the team was known as "The Pullets." They became the "Chicks" when the program was revived in 1974 before they thankfully morphed into the Lady Gamecocks.

Ed "Punky" Holler; Deacon Dan Reeves; Robert Neal "Pig"

GAMECOCKS

Gunter and Marion "Swamp" Swink were linemen on the 7-3 football team of 1925. Earl Clary, the Gaffney Ghost; Evelyn "Sweet E" Johnson; Steve "the Cadillac" Wadiak -- they're all part of Gamecock legend and lore.

Nicknames such as "Flick," bestowed on Gamecock basketball legend Alex English, are not slapped haphazardly upon individuals but rather reflect widely held perceptions about the person named. Proper names do that also.

Nowhere throughout history has this concept been more prevalent that in the Bible, where a name is not a mere label but is an expression of the essential nature of the named one. That is, a person's name reveals his or her character. Even God shares this concept; to know the name of God is to know God as he has chosen to reveal himself to us.

What does your name say about you? Honest, trustworthy, a seeker of the truth and a person of God? Or does the mention of your name cause your coworkers to whisper snide remarks, your neighbors to roll their eyes, or your friends to start making allowances for you?

Most importantly, what does your name say about you to God? He, too, knows you by name.

A good nickname inspires awe and ensures that you'll be enshrined in the Pantheon of [Sports] Legends.
-- Funny Sports Quotes Blog

Live so that your name evokes positive associations by people you know, the public, and God.

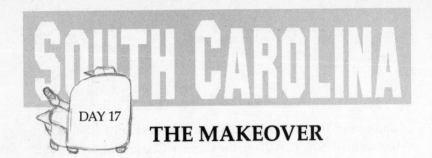
DAY 17

THE MAKEOVER

Read 2 Corinthians 5:11-21.

"If anyone is in Christ, he is a new creation; the old has gone, the new has come!" (v. 17)

Two-sport athletes often have to make themselves over as they move from one sport to another. Few, however, have ever had to remake themselves the way Ebony Jones did.

Jones was an all-state basketball player who drew interest from some smaller schools but decided to go to South Carolina for its nursing program. She stayed close to the game by becoming the Gamecock team manager.

Coach Susan Walvius soon noticed what a great attitude Jones had and how assertive she was in team huddles during games. So she encouraged Jones to walk on and play.

Jones was reluctant. "She was afraid of the getting-in-shape part," Walvius said. But she reconsidered and played in one game during the 2003-04 season. Once the season ended, her makeover began in earnest; through running and lifting weights, she dropped twenty pounds and worked herself into shape.

She became a fan favorite as the story circulated about the former manager who was now a player. "It was like icing on the cake when I'd go out there," Jones said, "and (the crowd) just exploded when I'd hit a shot." She saw only limited playing time, though, in both her sophomore and junior seasons. Still, Walvius placed her on scholarship prior to her senior season (2006-07).

When two of USC's guards went down with injuries, Jones was overnight not only an invaluable team member but a starter for six games. This manager-turned-starter averaged 14.2 minutes and 4.2 points per game for the 2006-07 season. Jones admitted that the first time Walvius told her she was starting, "I was like, 'Oh, my. I am?' It just totally caught me off guard."

Ebony Jones' younger teammates were quite surprised to learn she had started out as a manager so well had she made herself over into a Gamecock player.

Ever considered a makeover of your own? TV shows show us how changes in clothes, hair, and makeup and some weight loss can radically alter the way a person looks. But these changes are only skin deep. Even with a makeover, the real you — the person inside — remains unchanged. How can you make over that part of you?

By giving your heart and soul to Jesus -- just as you give up your hair to the makeover stylist. You won't look any different; you won't dance any better; you won't suddenly start talking smarter. The change is on the inside where you are brand new because the model for all you think and feel is now Jesus. He is the one you care about pleasing. Made over by Jesus, you realize that gaining his good opinion — not the world's — is all that really matters. And he isn't interested in how you look but how you act.

Don't think that the way you are today is the way you'll always be.
-- Vince Dooley

Jesus is the ultimate makeover artist; he can make you over without changing the way you look.

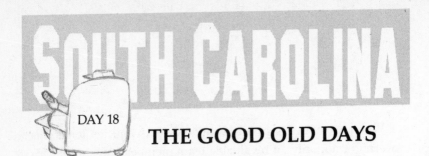
DAY 18

THE GOOD OLD DAYS

Read Psalm 102.

"My days vanish like smoke; . . . but you remain the same, and your years will never end" (vv. 3, 27).

Ah, the good old days when things were so different and much simpler. Coaching ten sports. No showers. No gymnasium. Such was the life of Coach Harry Parone in the good old days.

Parone played baseball and basketball for the University of South Carolina from 1946-49 after he served in World War II. Tom Price recounted Parone's adventures after graduation, when he was the athletics director and coach of all the sports at "tiny" Dentsville High School. He coached football, baseball, golf, boys and girls basketball, boys and girls track, boys tennis, girls volleyball, and soccer.

His locker room was in "a tar-paper shack" next to which the school kept some pigs. "Sometimes the odor was a little tough to take in the spring," Parone said. When the athletics program ran short of money, Parone would sell a pig.

That tar-paper locker room didn't have any showers, so Parone's athletes would sprint across the campus to another building to take a shower. "One lady who lived nearby complained to the principal about naked boys running across the school grounds. Sometimes I was one of them," Parone said.

He didn't have a fence around his football field, so admission to games was on the honor system. Parone would set up a table and charge 25 cents for students and 50 cents for adults. For the first five years of Parone's tenure, the school didn't have a gymnasium, so all the basketball games were played on the road. The team practiced on an outdoor court unless Parone could borrow the use of another school's court.

Parone, by the way, won three state football championships in those good old days.

It's a brutal truth that time just never stands still. The current of your life sweeps you along until you realize one day you've lived long enough to have a past. Part of it you cling to fondly. The stunts you pulled with your high-school buddies. Your first apartment. That dance with your first love. That special vacation. Those "good old days."

You hold on relentlessly to the memory of those old, familiar ways because of the stability they provide in our uncertain world. They will always be there even as times change and you age.

Another constant exists in your life too. God has been a part of every event in your life that created a memory because he was there. He's always there with you; the question is whether you ignore him or make him a part of your day.

A "good old day" is any day shared with God.

Years ago, you used to get out and fight and run around and chase each other with a jackhammer and stuff like that. Those were the good old days.

--Dale Earnhardt Jr., on NASCAR track etiquette

**Today is one of the "good old days"
if you share it with God.**

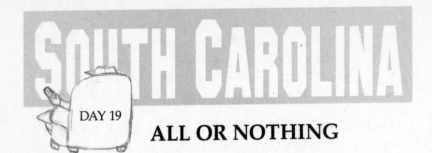

DAY 19

ALL OR NOTHING

Read Deuteronomy 6:4-9.

"Love the Lord your God with all your heart and with all your soul and with all your strength" (v. 5).

For legendary USC softball coach Joyce Compton, playing softball is a privilege born out of an all-or-nothing love for the game.

She has lived out that love in her life. Her marriage to the game was forged when she was 15 and tried out for an amateur women's softball team in New Jersey. She played college softball without a scholarship. After graduation, she played for an amateur team and then four seasons in the World Professional Softball Association. She earned $1,000 for 120 games a season.

Being accustomed to little pay and inadequate facilities served Compton well during her eleven seasons as a college coach in Connecticut and Missouri. As one writer put it, "Compton lived on her love for the game." She had to coach, drag the infield, and rake the baselines.

She came to USC in 1987 "as the team's only coach, with not much of a stadium," and promises of support. When USC moved to the SEC in 1992, however, softball in Columbia nearly died. At the time, the SEC didn't have softball, so the USC administration decided to kill the program.

Compton was not about to let the love of her life die without a fight. She launched a campaign that besieged USC officials. Even the Office of Civil Rights in Atlanta got into the act. The higher-

GAMECOCKS

ups at USC reinstated softball without missing a game.

Today, Compton is a Hall-of-Fame legend with more than 1,000 wins, and the USC softball program is one of the most successful in the nation. But if you come to play for Compton, you better come with talent and a passionate love for the game.

Throughout her life, Joyce Compton has stuck with softball and her teams no matter what happened. Many sports fans, though, cheer only when a team wins championships. They criticize or turn silent when losses and disappointments come. They're fair-weather fans.

True South Carolina fans stick with the Gamecocks no matter what, exactly the way God commands us to love him. Sure, this mandate is eons old, but the principle it established in our relationship with God has not changed. If anything, it has gained even more immediacy in our materialistic, secular culture that demands we love and worship anything and anybody but God.

Moreover, since God gave the original command, he has sent us Jesus. Thus, we today are even more indebted to God's grace and have even more reason to love God than did the Israelites to whom the original command was given.

God gave us everything; in return, we are to love him with everything we have and everything we are.

If you give everything you have, I don't care what the scoreboard says at the end of the game. In my book, we're gonna be winners.
-- *Coach Norman Dale in* Hoosiers

**With all we have and all we are –
that's the way we are to love God.**

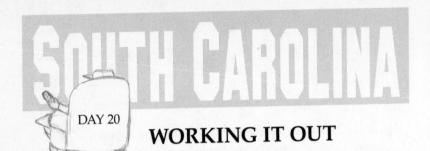
DAY 20

WORKING IT OUT

Read Matthew 9:35-38.

"Then he said to his disciples, 'The harvest is plentiful but the workers are few. Ask the Lord of the harvest, therefore, to send out workers into his harvest field'" (vv. 37-38).

Duce Staley is on any short list of the most gifted athletes ever to play for South Carolina. What made Staley stand out, however, was the extent to which he combined his talent with hard work.

Staley came to Columbia in 1995 as a junior after a stop at Itawamba (Miss.) Junior College. He had a breakout season in 1996, earning All-SEC honors. The Gamecocks went 6-5 under Brad Scott, and Staley led the SEC in rushing and finished 13th in the country with 1,116 yards, the fourth-highest single-season rushing total in Gamecock history. His two-year rushing totals at USC were 1,852 yards and 17 touchdowns. He had nine 100-yard rushing games, fourth best in USC history. Staley was also a versatile back with 59 receptions for 489 yards and two touchdowns and 26 kickoff returns for 566 yards.

While he obviously brought a bundle of raw talent with him to Columbia, Staley also arrived with a deep-seated work ethic. "What I learned in high school was how to work hard," he said. "Many athletes make it to the NFL and don't work hard anymore. I know you always have to work hard wherever you are or someone will pass you by."

Staley's hard work first made an impression on football

coaches when he was in the ninth grade and came over to the varsity practices after the B-team's season ended. "He enjoyed practices as much as games and would go full blast and bust it every play," one of his coaches said. Staley would volunteer to run the other team's offense. "He could have been sitting down, resting or saving himself . . . but he didn't," the coach said. "His work ethic and inner drive are remarkable."

His hard work and his talent drove Duce Staley all the way to stardom at USC and a pro career.

Do you embrace hard work or try to avoid it? No matter how hard you may try, you really can't escape hard work. Funny thing about all these labor-saving devices like cell phones and laptop computers: You're working longer and harder than ever. For many of us, our work defines us perhaps more than any other aspect of our lives. But there's a workforce you're a part of that doesn't show up in any Labor Department statistics or any IRS records.

You're part of God's staff; God has a specific job that only you can do for him. It's often referred to as a "calling," but it amounts to your serving God where there is a need in the way that best suits your God-given abilities and talents

You should stand ready to work for God all the time, 24-7. Those are awful hours, but the benefits are out of this world.

I've always believed that if you put in the work, the results will come.
— Michael Jordan

God calls you to work for him using the talents and gifts he gave you; whether you're a worker or a malingerer is up to you.

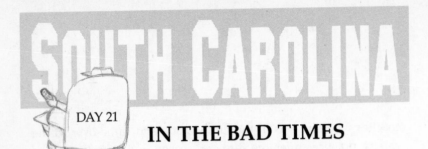

DAY 21

IN THE BAD TIMES

Read Philippians 1:3-14.

*"What has happened to me has really served to advance
the gospel. . . . Because of my chains, most of the brothers
in the Lord have been encouraged to speak the word of
God more courageously and fearlessly" (vv. 12, 14).*

I've been through hard times," Jon Coutlangus said during the
2002 baseball season.

His parents divorced when he was too young to remember,
and his father exited his life. He never even knew where his dad
lived. His mother died of cancer when he was 12.

In 2002, Coutlangus was hitting over .300 when he broke the
index finger on his left hand attempting to bunt against Arkansas.
He missed 22 games and should have missed more. Only a few
hours after he had pins removed from his finger, he suited up for
a game. "I couldn't bend my finger at all," he said. "It was like
hitting with one hand." He suffered through an 0-for-23 streak,
saw his average drop to .260, and was relegated to a position as a
late-inning defensive replacement.

But he never let any of it get him down, focusing instead on the
bright side. For instance, when his mother died, he went to live
with his grandparents. In 2003, they celebrated their 50th wedding
anniversary at Sarge Frye Field watching their grandson play
against Mississippi State. Coutlangus rejoiced that he was able to
play in the College World Series in 2002. "I could have been out

the whole rest of the season," he said.

As a senior in 2003, he was the starting centerfielder, hit. 317, and led the team in stolen bases. "I'm elated with the season Jon's had for us," Coach Ray Tanner said. "He's one of the most level players I've ever coached. . . . He's been a big key for us."

Jon Coutlangus knew the bad times in his life, but he chose not to dwell on them. Instead, he refused to let life get him down and made his major-league debut in 2007 with the Cincinnati Reds.

Loved ones die. You're downsized. Your biopsy appears cancerous. Your spouse could be having an affair. Hard, tragic times are an inevitable part of life.

This applies to Christians too. Faith in Jesus Christ does not exempt anyone from pain. Jesus promises he will be there for us to lead us through the valleys; he never promises that we will not enter them. The question therefore becomes how you handle the bad times. You can buckle to your knees in despair and cry, "Why me?" Or you can hit your knees in prayer and ask, "What do I do with this?"

Setbacks and tragedies are opportunities to reveal and to develop true character and abiding faith. Your faithfulness -- not your skipping merrily along through life without pain -- is what reveals the depth of your love for God.

If I were to say, "God, why me?" about the bad things, then I should have said, "God, why me?" about the good things that happened.
— Arthur Ashe

Faithfulness to God requires faith even in --
especially in -- the bad times.

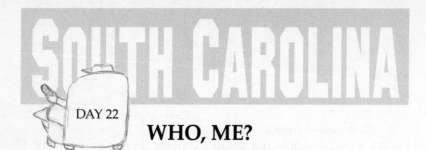
DAY 22

WHO, ME?

Read Judges 6:11-23.

"'But Lord,' Gideon asked, 'how can I save Israel? My clan is the weakest in Manasseh, and I am the least in my family'" (v. 15).

Brad Edwards was standing on the sideline minding his own business when a coach told him to get into the game and fill a position that he had no idea how to play.

Edwards was an All-American free safety as a senior in 1987, a two-year starter who led the team in tackles with 130 and interceptions with eight. He would go on to a nine-year professional career that would include a Super Bowl ring with the Redskins.

In 1984, though, he was a freshman who had little experience in the secondary and even less covering kickoffs, so he didn't expect to see any playing time in the season opener against The Citadel, especially after the game stayed close. South Carolina scored with a little more than a minute left to take a 31-24 lead, and that's when special teams coach Jim Washburn screamed for Edwards to go in on the kickoff as the contain guy.

Edwards' reaction was "Who, me?" "I had never really covered kicks," he said. So "a bewildered Edwards ran onto the field only vaguely aware of his assignment." He had no idea what to expect. "I didn't have a clue that other teams will sometimes put two or three men on the contain guy," he said. "All of a sudden a guy from The Citadel ear holes me out of nowhere. Their return guy

GAMECOCKS

is running free down the sideline, and I'm thinking, 'My career is over.'"

But Chris Major saved the game with a tackle at the Gamecock 23, and Otis Morris intercepted a pass with nine seconds left to clinch the win.

"Walking off the field, I just felt terrible," Edwards said. "It was like, 'You idiot freshman.' So that's how I got started."

You probably know how Brad Edwards felt when the coach called his name; you've experienced that gut-wrenching, sinking "who, me?" feeling.

How about that time the teacher called on you when you hadn't done a lick of homework? Or the night the hypnotist pulled you out of a room full of folks to be his guinea pig? You've had the wide-eyed look and the turmoil in your midsection when you were suddenly singled out and found yourself in a situation you neither sought nor were prepared for.

You may feel the same way Gideon did about being called to serve God in some way, quailing at the very notion of being audacious enough to teach Sunday school, lead a small group study, or coordinate a high school prayer club. After all, who's worthy enough to do anything like that?

The truth is that nobody is – but that doesn't seem to matter to God. And it's his opinion, not yours, that counts.

Surprise me.

> -- *Yogi Berra on where his wife should have him buried*

You're right in that no one is worthy to serve God, but the problem is that doesn't matter to God.

DAY 23

LIMITED-TIME OFFER

Read Psalm 103.

*"As for man, his days are like grass, he flourishes like a
flower of the field; the wind blows over it and it is gone.
. . . But from everlasting to everlasting the Lord's love is
with those who fear him" (vv. 15-17).*

Steve Wadiak was South Carolina's "first sports idol," the
school's "first mega-star athlete like no other before him on the
football field and a matinee idol." Only a few months after his
Gamecock playing days were over, though, he was dead.

Wadiak came to Columbia from Chicago in 1948 on the recommendation of a former player. He was described as "knock-down
good-looking" with "charm and a confidence about him that
wore well on others."

Wadiak shared playing time with Bishop Strickland in 1948,
but the field and the state were his after that. Against Clemson
in 1950, he "was branded forever as the greatest running back
in USC history," surpassing Earl Clary, who played from 1931-33.
On a muddy field, Wadiak rolled up 256 yards (a school record
that stood until Jeff Grantz broke it in 1973 with 260 yards) on 19
carries and scored two touchdowns as the Gamecocks tied the
heavily favored Tigers 14-14.

Nicknamed "The Cadillac," Wadiak in 1950 was unanimously
named the Southern Conference's Player of the Year and was
All-America. Against George Washington, he set a school record

that still stands with a 96-yard touchdown run from scrimmage. He finished his career with 2,878 yards, a school record that stood until George Rogers broke it in 1980.

He was drafted by the Pittsburgh Steelers in January 1952; the future was bright. On the night of March 9, however, Steve Wadiak was the only one of six passengers to die when the car he was in left the road at about 90 miles an hour.

A heart attack, cancer, or an accident will probably take -- or has already taken -- someone you know or love who is "too young to die" such as Steve Wadiak.

The death of a younger person never seems to "make sense." That's because such a death belies the common view of death as the natural end of a life lived well and lived long. Moreover, you can't see the whole picture as God does, so you can't know how the death furthers God's kingdom.

At such a time, you can seize the comforting truth that God is in control and therefore everything will be all right one day. You can also gain a sense of urgency in your own life by appreciating that God's offer of life through Jesus Christ is a limited-time offer that expires at your death – and there's no guarantee about when that will be.

No one knows when is going to die, so if we're going to accept Christ, we'd better not wait, because death can come in the blink of an eye.
-- Bobby Bowden

God offers you life through Jesus Christ, but you must accept the offer before your death, which is when it expires.

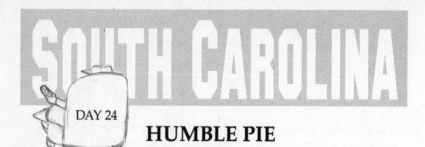
HUMBLE PIE

Read Matthew 23:1-12.

"The greatest among you will be your servant. For whoever exalts himself will be humbled, and whoever humbles himself will be exalted" (vv. 11-12).

Grady Wallace didn't like to talk too much about his exploits at South Carolina.

For instance, asked about a personal highlight of his basketball career with the Gamecocks, he mentioned the 84-81 win over Duke in the 1957 ACC Tournament. "They were up by a substantial margin, and we made a little push in the second half and won," he said. Bob Fulton, the longtime USC announcer, said that account was true, but it lacked a few important details. "Basically, Grady stood in the corner and tore the nets down," Fulton said.

In fact, Wallace scored the Gamecocks' last 14 points in a 41-point night. He pulled off an old-fashioned three-point play to put USC in front 82-81 with 20 seconds to play and then wrapped up the deal with two free throws. He finished his senior season with a scoring average of 31.3 points per game, which led the nation, ahead of, among others, Elgin Baylor and Wilt Chamberlain.

Wallace played for Carolina for two seasons. In addition to leading the nation in scoring, he led the ACC in rebounding in 1957, set the school record (since broken) of 54 points in a game, and closed out his career in Columbia with 44 points and 20 rebounds in his final game. He averaged 23.9 points per game in 1956 to give him 1,456 points in his two seasons. His career scoring average of 28.0 points per game is still the school record.

"I loved basketball," Wallace said, talking about the game and not himself. "But setting records? I never thought about that. I just wanted to play." And play he did. He just wouldn't brag about it.

We fail to make a sports team or a cheerleading squad. Our children remind us what fossils we are. There's always somebody younger, smarter, better looking, and more aggressive around. Sometimes it's not very hard being humble, is it?

But Jesus said that humility is to be a way of life, and then he demonstrated what he meant by the way he lived. Humility doesn't demand abject poverty, ongoing afflictions, or a complete lack of social status. Humility, rather, is an attitude toward God and other people.

God calls us in Jesus to be willing servants, always looking for the chance to help others. We banish both thoughts and acts of violence, arrogance, and selfish pride toward others, replacing them with a lifestyle that values peace and harmony.

This is certainly not the way society usually thinks and functions. Moreover, in Jesus' topsy-turvy kingdom, today's servants are tomorrow's exalted.

Mental toughness is humility because it behooves all of us to remember that simplicity is the sign of greatness and meekness is the sign of strength.

-- Vince Lombardi

**To be humbled today in the name of Jesus
is to be exalted forever in the presence of Jesus.**

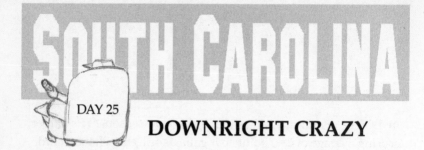

SOUTH CAROLINA

DAY 25

DOWNRIGHT CRAZY

Read Luke 13:31-35.

"Some Pharisees came to Jesus and said to him, 'Leave this place and go somewhere else. Herod wants to kill you.' He replied, 'Go tell that fox . . . I must keep going today and tomorrow and the next day'" (vv. 31-33).

You're nuts."

That was the general reaction to an idea real estate developer Ed Robinson had in 1990 that today is such an iconic part of South Carolina football that other schools are copying it. Robinson's crazy idea was the Cockaboose Railroad.

Robinson decided something needed to be done with the ugly vacant railroad tracks behind the south side of Williams-Brice Stadium. He had the brilliant if bizarre notion that they could be used to give Carolina boosters a luxurious tailgating site. In two years of feverish work, he purchased the tracks and 22 old cabooses, parked them on the tracks, and secured approval from the city for construction of sewer lines. When that was done, he set out to sell the cabooses – which at the time were simply gutted steel boxes in need of a paint job -- to prominent and wealthy Carolina boosters.

The reaction he received was always the same. "People would look at you, and they would give you this kind of wild-eyed look, like, 'You're nuts,'" Robinson said. "Then they'd say, 'Yeah. I want one.'" Robinson sold all the cabooses in two days.

Bob David purchased one of those original 22 cabooses, but as Robinson did, he ran into some incredulity. "When my mother first heard about this, she flat out told me, 'That is the stupidest thing you've ever done,'" David said.

The Cockaboose Railroad has become "kind of an icon for Carolina football," said USC Athletics Director Mike McGee. "It's become one of those things that identifies Carolina."

And when Ed Robinson started out, folks just thought the whole idea was downright crazy.

What some see as downright crazy sometimes turns out to be shrewd instead. Like Ed Robinson and his Cockabooses. Or like the time you went into business for yourself or when you decided to go back to school. Maybe it was when you fixed up that old house. Or when you bought that new company's stock.

You know a good thing when you see it but are also shrewd enough to spot something that's downright crazy. Jesus was that way too. He knew that entering Jerusalem was in complete defiance of all apparent reason and logic since a whole bunch of folks who wanted to kill him were waiting for him there.

Nevertheless, he went because he also knew that when the great drama had played out he would defeat not only his personal enemies but the most fearsome enemy of all: death itself. It was, after all, a shrewd move that provided the way to your salvation.

Football is easy if you're crazy.

-- Bo Jackson

It's so good it sounds crazy -- but it's not: through faith in Jesus, you can have eternal life with God.

DAY 26

AS A RULE

Read Luke 5:27-32.

*"Why do you eat and drink with tax collectors and
'sinners'?" (v. 30b)*

Confusion over the rules once contributed to South Carolina's
participation in what may well be the longest, slowest game in
college football history.

The rules governing the college football at the beginning of
the twentieth century were constantly changing as the game
evolved. South Carolina's first game was in 1892 (See devotion
No. 1.), but not until the 1912 season was the field reduced from
110 yards to 100 with the creation of the ten-yard end zone as we
know it today. That was also the season in which the value of a
touchdown was increased to six points and teams were allowed
four downs – instead of three – to make a first down. These rule
changes followed an earlier round in 1910 when crawling and aiding the ball carrier by pulling or pushing him were outlawed.
The changes also established the neutral zone that created the
line of scrimmage and set the length of a quarter at 15 minutes.

With those new rules in place, South Carolina began the 1910
season against the College of Charleston. The weather was awful:
"The rain plummeted down. The field was in deplorable condition
and the game was a punting battle."

The miserable weather itself made the game interminably long
for the few spectators who braved it out, but the game was contin-

ually stopped "while officials consulted the rulebook since both teams were unfamiliar with the new rules."

"It had to be the longest game on record," the *Gamecock* lamented. "It started just after mid-day and was not concluded until nearly sundown."

Though few really cared by the time it was over, South Carolina won 8-0.

Like the South Carolina football players, you live by rules others set up. Some lender determined the interest rate on your mortgage and your car loan. You work hours and shifts somebody else established. Someone else decided what day your garbage gets picked up and what school district your house is in.

Jesus encountered societal rules also, including those that dictated what company he should keep, what people, in other words, were fit for him to socialize with, talk to, or share a meal with. Jesus ignored the rules, choosing love instead and demonstrating his disdain for society's rules by mingling with the outcasts, the lowlifes, the poor, and the misfits.

You, too, have to choose when you find yourself in the presence of someone whom society deems undesirable. Will you choose the rules or will you opt for love?

I believe in rules. Sure I do. If there weren't any rules, how could you break them?

-- Leo Durocher

Society's rules dictate who is acceptable and who is not, but love in the name of Jesus knows no such distinctions.

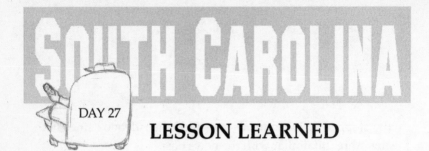

DAY 27

LESSON LEARNED

Read Matthew 11:20-30.

"Take my yoke upon you and learn from me" (v. 29).

Coaches praised Syvelle Newton's intelligence that enabled him to become one of the most versatile players in USC football history. He even learned a lesson from a horrible athletic injury.

As a senior in 2006, Newton played quarterback, wide receiver, and defensive back. He started the first nine games at quarterback, but when Coach Steve Spurrier went to Blake Mitchell down the stretch, the coaches wanted to find some way to keep the athletic Newton on the field. So he moved to free safety for the first time ever. "The first thing I noticed (when Newton switched over to defense)," said Gamecock defensive coordinator Tyrone Nix, "was that he's a very intelligent young man, and he picks up on things almost instantly."

That intelligence and versatility enabled Newton to leave USC as one of only four players in college football history with more than 600 yards rushing, passing, and receiving in his career.

That put him squarely in the company of two other USC players who were renowned for their versatility: Alex Hawkins and Sterling Sharpe. Hawkins was the ACC Player of the Year in 1958 as a Gamecock running back who also started at defensive back. In the NFL, he played cornerback, halfback, fullback, split end, flanker, and tight end. Sharpe was an All-American receiver in 1987 who also returned kickoffs and played some at running back, taking five to six pitchouts a game.

As the coaches said, Newton learned quickly. He even learned a valuable lesson in the 2005 season when he blew out an Achilles tendon against Vanderbilt. "I believe I was being too overconfident, and not giving God enough credit for what He has done for me," Newton said, turning the devastating injury into a blessing.

Lesson learned.

Learning about anything in life requires a combination of education and experience. Education is the accumulation of facts that we call knowledge; experience is the acquisition of wisdom and discernment, which add purpose and understanding to our knowledge.

The most difficult way to learn is trial and error: dive in blindly and mess up. The best way to learn is through example coupled with a set of instructions: Someone has gone ahead to show you the way and has written down all the information you need to follow.

In teaching us the way to live godly lives, God chose the latter method. He set down in his book the habits, actions, and attitudes that make for a way of life in accordance with his wishes. He also sent us Jesus to explain and to illustrate.

God teaches us not just how to exist but how to live. We just need to be attentive students.

It's what you learn after you know it all that counts.

— John Wooden

To learn from Jesus is to learn what life is all about and how God means for us to live it.

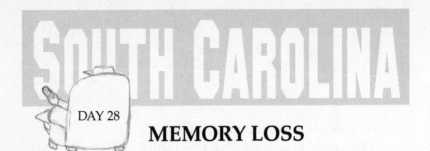

DAY 28

MEMORY LOSS

Read 1 Corinthians 11:17-29.

"[D]o this in remembrance of me" (v. 24).

The team that time has forgotten," one writer called them.

The team captain agreed. "We're the best-kept secret at Carolina," Buck Smith, then 94, said in 2005 before he added, "Nobody knows."

Once upon a time before the Frank McGuire era, a Gamecock team "set the school standard for basketball excellence." The Gamecocks won 32 straight games over two seasons and claimed the school's first conference title. The 1933 Gamecocks won their last fifteen games including the Southern Conference Tournament title. They then won their first seventeen games of the 1934 season before an epidemic of the mumps felled them.

"Those two seasons, we ranked among the top four teams in the country," Smith said. "We could play. For that time, we had a heckuva ball club."

The teams were labeled the Tall Texans. There were four of them who formed the heart of the two-year run: brothers Freddie and Bennie Tompkins, Dana Henderson, and John Rowland. They came to Carolina as a package deal.

Traveling in a bus that belonged to the college glee club, the team opened the 1934 season with four games on the road. They whipped Presbyterian 84-9 and then cruised past N.C. State, Duke, and North Carolina on successive nights.

GAMECOCKS

They went 17-0 until two starters were felled by the mumps and they lost in the opening round of the Southern Conference Tournament. They then proved they were the best in the country by whipping Pittsburgh in a battle of No. 1 and No. 2.

The record was 35-3 over two seasons; yes, they could play, this team that time has forgotten.

Memory makes us who we are. Whether our memories are dreams or nightmares, they shape us and to a large extent determine our actions and reactions. Alzheimer's is so terrifying because it steals our memory from us and in the process we lose ourselves. We disappear.

The greatest tragedy of our lives is that God remembers. In response to that memory, he condemns us for our sin. On the other hand, the greatest joy of our lives is that God remembers. In response to that memory, he came as Jesus to wash even the memory of our sins away.

Through memory, we encounter revival. At the Last Supper, Jesus instructed his disciples and us to remember. In sharing this unique meal with fellow believers and remembering Jesus and his actions, we meet Christ again not just as a memory but as an actual living presence.

To remember is to keep our faith alive.

I don't want them to forget Babe Ruth. I just want them to remember Hank Aaron.

-- Hank Aaron

**We remember Jesus,
and God will not remember our sins.**

DAY 29

BIRDS OF A FEATHER

Read Genesis 6:11-22; 8:1-4.

"God remembered Noah and all the wild animals and the livestock that were with him in the ark" (v. 8:1).

Bulldogs and Tigers and the like – they're as common as South Carolina touchdowns. But only one major college has the Gamecocks.

It didn't start out that way. In 1892, when the students of South Carolina College voted on a mascot, they selected the Jaguars. So it remained until the 1902 season, which was the first under the Gamecock banner. The nickname arose from a newspaper story that said the South Carolina players "fought like gamecocks" against Clemson, a 12-6 win. This was certainly a most flattering comparison since gamecocks "are known for their courage in battle and willingness to fight to the death."

The nickname was actually written "Game Cocks" until the *State* shortened the name to one word. The nickname "became unofficially official" during the 1902 game against Furman. Late in the first half, a Furman student ran onto the field with a stuffed rooster, plucking the tail feathers much to the delight of the Furman fans. They began to shout, "Poor little gamecock, poor little gamecock." So it would forever be.

The use of the feisty fighting bird as a mascot presented something of a quandary with the rise of women's intercollegiate sports in the 1970s. The gamecock is a male bird. Women's

GAMECOCKS

basketball was the sport with the highest profile from the outset, and appreciating the situation, the players called themselves the "Carolina Chicks." Helen Timmermans, the school's first Associate Director of Athletics for Women, even had a vanity license plate that read "Chicks." After a while, though, the consensus arose among the women that the name "Chicks" was degrading, so the women's teams became the "Lady Gamecocks," male bird or no.

Do you have a dog or two around the place? How about a cat that passes time staring longingly at your caged canary? Kids have gerbils? Maybe you've gone more exotic with a tarantula or a ferret.

Americans love our pets; in fact, more households in this country have pets than have children. We not only share our living space with animals we love and protect but also with some – such as roaches and rats – that we seek to exterminate.

None of us, though, has the problems Noah faced when he packed God's menagerie into one boat. God saved all his varmints from extinction, including the fish and the ducks, who were probably quite delighted with the whole flood business.

The lesson is clear for us who strive to live as God would have us: All living things are under God's care. It isn't just our cherished pets that God calls us to care for and respect; we are to serve God as stewards of all of his creatures.

A gamecock is a fighting rooster known for its spirit and courage.
-- www.GamecocksOnline.com

God cares about all his creatures,
and he expects us to respect them too.

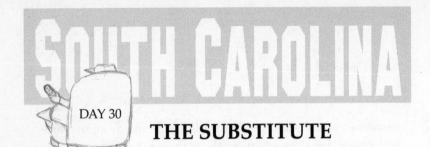

DAY 30

THE SUBSTITUTE

Read Galatians 3:10-14.

"Christ redeemed us from the curse of the law by becoming a curse for us" (v. 13).

Because head coach June Raines substituted for himself, the South Carolina baseball team had a dramatic win in the College World Series.

The 1977 team was one of South Carolina's greatest. Outfielder Mookie Wilson and pitcher Randy Martz (See Devotion No. 9.) were All-Americas, and pitcher Blake Moore was a freshman All-America. Martz was the national Player of the Year. Seven players signed pro contracts. The team went 43-12-1 and was the national runner-up.

Against Baylor in the opening round of the 1977 College World Series, the score was tied after nine innings, but Baylor scored a run in the top of the tenth. In the bottom of the inning, second baseman Mark Van Bever led off with a double and advanced to third on a ground out. Next up was senior leftfielder Chuck McLean, only a .260 hitter but one of Raines' favorites because he was so competitive. Raines liked to have McLean at the plate when the game was on the line, and this was one of those times.

Sure enough, McLean scorched a line drive over the center-fielder's head with Van Bever scoring easily. McLean set a school record for a career with nine triples, and he left the batter's box with a triple on his mind. But as he neared third, assistant coach

Johnny Hunton waved him home. McLean beat the throw for a game-ending inside-the-park home run.

Hunton had relieved Raines as third-base coach in the inning, and Raines later admitted he would have held McLean at third if he had still been coaching. The Gamecocks might well have won the game anyway, but the substitution made it a sure thing.

Wouldn't it be cool if you had a substitute for all of life's hard stuff? Telling of a death in the family? Call in your sub. Breaking up with your boyfriend? Job interview? Chemistry test? Crucial presentation at work? Time out! Bring the sub into the game and let him handle it.

We do have such a substitute, but not for the matters of life. Instead, Jesus is our substitute for matters of life and death. Since Jesus has already made it, we don't have to make the sacrifice God demands for forgiveness and salvation.

One of the ironies of our age is that many people desperately grope for a substitute for Jesus. Mysticism, human philosophies such as Scientology, false religions such as Hinduism and Islam, cults, New Age approaches that preach self-fulfillment without responsibility or accountability – they and others like them are all pitiful, inadequate substitutes for Jesus.

Accept no substitutes. It's Jesus or nothing.

I never substitute just to substitute. The only way a guy gets off the floor is if he dies.
— Former basketball coach Abe Lemons

There is no substitute for Jesus,
the consummate substitute.

DAY 31

CONFIDENCE MAN

Read Micah 7:5-7.

"As for me, I will look to the Lord, I will wait for the God of my salvation" (v. 7 NRSV).

Gamecock cornerback Fred Bennett was such a confident player that he promised to get the ball back for his quarterback – and did so on the very next play.

Bennett was a two-time All-SEC player who had 108 tackles and nine interceptions while he was in Columbia. He was taken by the Houston Texans in the fourth round of the 2007 NFL Draft.

On the night of Saturday, Oct. 2, 2004, the Gamecocks were in Tuscaloosa trying to shake the hallowed halls of Bryant-Denny Stadium by coming away with a win. They led 6-3 in the third quarter but appeared to be in trouble after sophomore quarterback Syvelle Newton threw an interception.

Newton's head was hanging as he trotted off the field. That's when Bennett made his promise. "Pick your head up," Bennett told Newton. "I'm fixing to get the ball back for you."

Sure enough, on Alabama's next play from scrimmage, Bennett picked off a pass. That interception ignited a series of events that culminated in one of the most storied wins in Gamecock history. In the two minutes and 11 seconds after Bennett's interception, South Carolina picked off another pass and Newton scored a pair of touchdowns on the ground. The shellshocked Crimson Tide never recovered and lost 20-3.

For the night, Bennett had a pair of interceptions while cornerback Tremaine Tyler and freshman Ko Simpson each picked off a Bama pass. Bennett attributed the success to preparation. "I thought their quarterbacks were telegraphing their passes. We were ready for it," he said.

Ready enough – and confident enough – to promise an interception. And deliver.

You need confidence in all areas of your life. You're confident the company you work for will pay you on time, or you wouldn't go to work. You turn the ignition confident your car will start. When you flip a switch, you expect the light co come on.

Confidence in other people and in things is often misplaced, though. Companies go broke; car batteries die; light bulbs burn out. Even the people you love the most sometimes let you down.

So where can you place your trust with absolute confidence you won't be betrayed? In the promises of God.

Such confidence is easy, of course, when everything's going your way, but what about when you cry as Micah did, "What misery is mine!" As Micah says, that's when your confidence in God must be its strongest. That's when you wait, confident that God will not fail you, that he will never let you down.

When it gets right down to the wood-chopping, the key to winning is confidence.

-- College football coach Darrell Royal

People, things, and organizations will let you down; only God can be trusted absolutely and confidently.

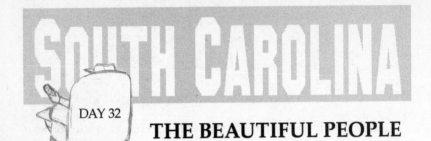

DAY 32

THE BEAUTIFUL PEOPLE

Read Matthew 23:23-28.

"Woe to you, teachers of the law and Pharisees, you hypocrites! You are like whitewashed tombs, which look beautiful on the outside, but on the inside are full of dead men's bones and everything unclean" (v. 27).

Recruiting is bewildering business -- except in the case of Alex Hawkins. All it took was clean air, clear water, and a pretty girl.

Hawkins is one of South Carolina's greatest players ever. He played halfback from 1956-58 and as a senior in 1958 was named the ACC Player of the Year and a third-team All-America. He went on to a ten-year NFL career, mostly with the Baltimore Colts.

Growing up in Charleston, WV, Hawkins gravitated toward athletics because "there was absolutely nothing else to do. . . . We never had a car to go anywhere where there might have been more going on." Hawkins excelled in football, basketball, and baseball. A guy from Kentucky told Hawkins they'd give him "$200 a month, clothes, and a farm" if he'd play basketball for the Wildcats. Hawkins told the coach he didn't want to be a farmer and scratched Kentucky off his list.

Hawkins ultimately decided on football, and most folks figured he was a cinch for the West Virginia Mountaineers. But Hawkins wanted to leave his home state. "It was a shrinking state when I was there," he explained.

South Carolina was among the schools recruiting Hawkins,

and one trip south convinced him. "They took me water skiing with this really pretty girl," he remembered. "I was thinking, 'clean air, clear water, and pretty girls.'" South Carolina was the place for him.

Once he got to Columbia, though, "I never did see that girl again."

Remember the brunette who sat behind you in history class? Or the blonde in English? And how about that hunk from the next apartment who washes his car every Saturday morning and just forces you to get outside earlier than you really want to?

We do love those beautiful people.

It is worth remembering amid our adulation of superficial beauty that *Vogue* or *People* probably wouldn't have been too enamored of Jesus' looks. Isaiah 53 declares that our savior "had no beauty or majesty to attract us to him, nothing in his appearance that we should desire him."

Though Jesus never urged folks to walk around with body odor and unwashed hair, he did admonish us to avoid being overly concerned with physical beauty, which fades with age despite tucks and Botox. What matters to God is inner beauty, which reveals itself in the practice of justice, mercy, and faith, and which is not only lifelong but eternal.

Ah, the glories of women's sports: the camaraderie. The quiet dignity. The proud refusal to buy into traditional stereotypes of beauty.
-- Sports Illustrated for Women

**When it comes to looking good to God,
it's what's inside that counts.**

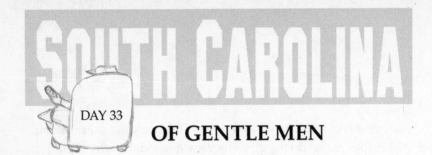

OF GENTLE MEN

Read John 2:13-22.

"He made a whip out of cords, and drove all from the temple area . . .; he scattered the coins of the money changers and overturned their tables" (v. 15).

James A. "Buck" Freeman was such a gentleman that in more than forty years as a college basketball coach, he received only one technical foul.

Freeman looked every inch the gentleman that he was. He was "a lifelong bachelor, distinguished looking, with a mane of white hair" and the "father figure to countless intramural student-athletes as well as varsity stars."

Freeman was 27 when he graduated from St. John's University in 1927 and became the school's head basketball coach. Among his players was Frank McGuire. In ten seasons, his record was 179-32. He was an innovative coach, introducing switching defenses and the use of screens in offensive patterns. Eventually he joined McGuire at North Carolina and eventually followed him on to South Carolina as an assistant and advisor.

Before Carolina Coliseum was constructed, he often kept the old Carolina Field House open until the wee hours of the morning because students still wanted to play. He followed a daily routine, this courtly gentleman. He lived in the Heart of Columbia Hotel and in the evening would stop at the Capitol News Stand on Main Street, buy several newspapers, and head back to his room, stopping under the streetlights to read.

The only technical foul of Freeman's career came in December 1965 against Duke, a game USC won 73-71. The technical foul embarrassed Freeman so much that he apologized for it.

Health forced Freeman's retirement in 1973, and he died only eight months later, a gentleman who also happened to be, as McGuire said, "one of the greatest basketball coaches of all time."

A calm, caring manner and a soft voice are often mistaken for weakness, and gentle men are frequently misunderstood by those who fail to appreciate their inner strength. But Buck Freeman's coaching career and Jesus' rampage through the Jerusalem temple illustrate the perils of underestimating a determined gentleman.

A gentleman treats other people kindly, respectfully, and justly, and conducts himself ethically in all situations. A gentleman doesn't lack resolve or backbone. Instead, he determines to live in a way that is exceedingly difficult in our selfish, me-first society; he lives the lifestyle God desires for us all.

Included in that mode of living is the understanding that the best way to have a request honored is to make it civilly, with a smile. God works that way too. He could bully you and boss you around; you couldn't stop him. But instead, he gently requests your attention, waiting for the courtesy of a reply.

Play to win, observe the rules, and act like a gentleman.
-- Basketball coach and author Clair Bee

God is a gentleman, soliciting your attention
politely and then patiently waiting for you
to give him the courtesy of a reply.

DAY 34

THE MOTHER LODE

Read John 19:25-30.

"Near the cross of Jesus stood his mother" (v. 25).

It's a gene thing," Cristina Ciocan said about her specialty on the basketball court. She got it from her mama.

Ciocan is the career assist leader for South Carolina women's basketball (615), leading the team in assists all four years she played (2000-04). She holds the USC women's single game assist record of 18 against Florida A&M in 2003. Her 14 assists against Vanderbilt in 2002 is the second-highest total for a single game in Gamecock history.

Ciocan was downright unusual in her approach to the game. While others consulted the stat sheet to look at points and rebounds, Ciocan looked first to the assist column and second to the turnover column. Her game focused on the assist-to-turnover ratio.

That slightly different attitude was no accident, however; it was genetic. Her mother played ten seasons for the Romanian National Team and coached the Junior National Team. "There were a few years when she was considered the best passer in Europe," Ciocan said of her mom. "She was the first one to teach me the game. She taught me the basics." Thus when mother and daughter talked on the phone before and after every USC game, the conversation centered on assists and turnovers.

Ciocan was a natural point guard, but it wasn't her natural

position. In Romania, she played wing or inside, and she was reluctant to accept Coach Susan Walvius' plan to play the point. Before long, though, the "gregarious redhead [thought] nothing of flinging the ball the length of the court" in hopes of an easy basket. Her teammates ran the court because they knew Ciocan would find them.

Just as her mama taught her.

Mamas often do the sort of thing Cristina Ciocan's mother did for her: teach their children and help them make the most of their talents. No mother in history, though, has faced a challenge to match that of Mary, whom God chose to be the mother of Jesus. Like mamas and their children throughout time, Mary experienced both joy and perplexity in her relationship with her son.

To the end, though, Mary stood by her boy. She followed him all the way to his execution, an act of love and bravery since Jesus was condemned as an enemy of the Roman Empire.

But just as mothers like Mary, Cristina Ciocan's, and perhaps yours would apparently do anything for their children, so will God do anything out of love for his children. After all, that was God on the cross at the foot of which Mary stood, and he was dying for you, one of his children.

Everyone should find time to write and to go see their mother. I think that's healthy.

— Bear Bryant

**Mamas often sacrifice for their children,
but God too will do anything out of love
for his children, including dying on a cross.**

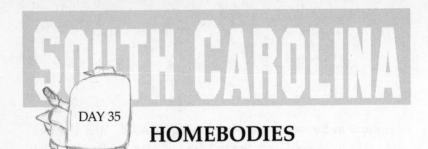

DAY 35

HOMEBODIES

Read 2 Corinthians 5:1-10.

"We . . . would prefer to be away from the body and at home with the Lord" (v. 8).

Tom Addison couldn't find a home.

Addison was an offensive lineman and a star linebacker for USC from 1955-57. He was inducted into the South Carolina Athletic Hall of Fame in 2004.

He was drafted by the Baltimore Colts in 1958 but was a late cut and returned to Columbia to complete his degree and help coach the freshman football team. He tried the pros again in 1959 and spent a season on the Philadelphia Eagles' taxi squad. He got a real job after that, figuring his football playing days were over.

But the American Football League was organizing and needed players, and the Eagles called Addison and told him they had cut a deal to send some players to something called the Denver Broncos. Addison's reaction was, "The Denver What?" He was convinced he could still play, though, so he joined the Denver team in New Jersey before a game against the New York Titans. "I thought I was on the squad," Addison said.

That's when his downright comic whirlwind tour of professional football began in earnest.

Just before the game on Friday night, Addison learned he had been traded to the Buffalo Bills. "I got there too late for their game that week and I asked for an advance on my salary," Addison re-

GAMECOCKS

called. "They said no, they couldn't pay me until I played."

So he suited up for his third team in less than a week when to his dismay he discovered he had been traded yet again – to the-then Boston Patriots. The team had a week off, so Addison had to send home for money so he could eat.

After all that moving around that Addison called "absolutely ridiculous," he found a home with the Patriots. He was a five-time AFL all-star and was widely considered the league's best linebacker until a knee injury in 1966 ended his career.

Addison then came back to South Carolina to make his home.

Home is not necessarily a matter of geography. It may be that place you share with your spouse and your children, whether it's Boston or Alaska. You may feel at home when you return to Columbia, wondering why you were so eager to leave in the first place. Maybe the home you grew up in still feels like an old shoe, a little worn but comfortable and inviting.

God planted that sense of home in us because he is a God of place and our place is with him. Thus, we may live a few blocks away from our parents and grandparents or we may relocate every few years, but we still will sometimes feel as though we don't really belong no matter where we are. We don't; our true home is with God in the place Jesus has gone ahead to prepare for us. We are homebodies and we are perpetually homesick.

Everybody's better at home.

– Basketball player Justin Dentmon

**We are continually homesick for our real home,
which is with God in Heaven.**

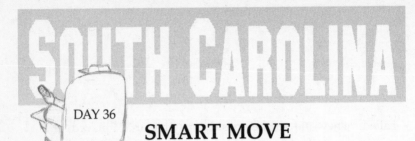
DAY 36

SMART MOVE

Read 1 Kings 4:29-34; 10:23-11:4.

"King Solomon was greater in riches and wisdom than all the other kings of the earth. The whole world sought audience with Solomon to hear the wisdom God had put in his heart" (vv. 10:23-24).

A completely boneheaded play by one of South Carolina's greatest players ever turned into one of the greatest plays ever.

Bobby Bryant arrived in Columbia in 1963, so tall and so thin that his nickname was "Bones." He never weighed more than 172 pounds his entire football career. He played baseball and football for three varsity seasons; his senior year he was first-team All-ACC in both sports and was named the conference's top athlete.

Bryant chose football over baseball after he left South Carolina. He had a 14-year career with the Minnesota Vikings that included two Pro Bowls and four Super Bowls. He set a club record with 50 career interceptions.

Bryant's senior year in Columbia (1966) was Paul Dietzel's first year as head coach, and the season was a nightmare. The Gamecocks won only one game, but a play Bryant made was the key to that lone win. Years later he said the play was his biggest thrill as a Gamecock and that the whole play was a mistake on his part.

Dietzel insisted his punt returners not field any ball inside the 10-yard line. Against N.C. State, the Wolfpack led until a second-quarter punt. Bryant was back to receive the punt, and to Dietzel's horror, he apparently mistook the goal line for the ten, fielded the football on a high bounce at the two, and headed upfield. He got a couple of key blocks, broke into the clear around the 30, and wound up with the longest punt return in school history. The 98-yard touchdown jump-started the 31-21 Gamecock win.

And it was a play that wasn't a smart move at all.

Remember that time you wrecked the car when you spilled hot coffee on your lap? That cold morning you fell out of the boat? The time you gave your honey a tool box for her birthday?

Formal education notwithstanding, we all make some dumb moves sometime because time spent in a classroom is not an accurate gauge of common sense. Folks impressed with their own smarts often grace us with erudite pronouncements that we intuitively recognize as flawed, unworkable, or simply wrong.

A good example is the observation that great intelligence and scholarship are not compatible with faith in God. That is, the more you know, the less you believe. But any incompatibility occurs only because we begin to trust in our own wisdom rather than the wisdom of God. We forget, as Solomon did, that God is the ultimate source of all our knowledge and wisdom and that even our ability to learn is a gift from God.

Not smart at all.

I don't hire anybody not brighter than I am. If they're not smarter than me, I don't need them.

-- *Bear Bryant*

Being truly smart means trusting in God's wisdom rather than only in your own knowledge.

DAY 37

THE PIONEER SPIRIT

Read Luke 5:1-11.

"So they pulled their boats up on shore, left everything and followed him" (v. 11).

I just look at myself as a golfer," Erica Battle said. But when she was at South Carolina, she was much more.

Battle was a consistent performer on the Gamecock women's golf team from 2002-06. She was outstanding enough to compete as the only freshman on the 2002-03 squad and as a senior to win the prestigious Dinah Shore Trophy, presented to "the best golfer in the nation in terms of success on the golf course, success in the classroom, community service and extraordinary leadership."

She was also the first African-American – man or woman -- to play golf for USC and the only African-American golfer – male or female – in the SEC at that time.

"When I do have minorities come up and tell me how much I've impacted them . . ., it makes me realize I'm not out there only to play golf sometimes," Battle said of the responsibility she knew she carried. "I'm out there representing my race, also."

She learned the game from her father when she was 7. She got tired of tagging along at his golf outings, so she decided she would show him how to play. When she was 15, she was the ladies' club champion and got the prime parking spot that accompanied the title. "It was funny," said her mother, Daphne, "because I don't think she could drive at the time."

GAMECOCKS

When Gamecocks coach Kristi Coggins recruited Battle, she told Battle she could be "the female Tiger." She had the "opportunity to be different and achieve some things that people before her haven't achieved," Coggins said. "And that's something that I think she sees as a challenge and really a reality for herself."

The reality was that South Carolina Gamecock Erica Battle was a pioneer and a trailblazer.

Going to a place in your life you've never been before requires a willingness to take risks and face uncertainty head-on. You may have never blazed a trail at a major college, but you've had your moments when your latent pioneer spirit manifested itself. That time you changed careers, ran a marathon, volunteered at a homeless shelter, learned Spanish, or went back to school.

While attempting new things invariably begets apprehension, the truth is that when life becomes too comfortable and too familiar, it gets boring. The same is true of God, who is downright dangerous because he calls us to be anything but comfortable as we serve him. He summons us to continually blaze new trails in our faith life, to follow him no matter what. Stepping out on faith is risky all right, but the reward is a life of accomplishment, adventure, and joy that cannot be equaled anywhere else.

Life is an adventure. I wouldn't want to know what's going to happen next.

-- Bobby Bowden

Unsafe and downright dangerous, God calls us out of the place where we are comfortable to a life of adventure and trailblazing in his name.

DAY 38

GIFT-WRAPPED

Read James 1:12-18.

"Every good and perfect gift is from above, coming down from the Father of the heavenly lights" (v. 17).

Corey Atkins and the Gamecocks got a gift from the refs, and they weren't about to return it.

Atkins was a sophomore outside linebacker in 1997 when the Gamecocks opened their season against Central Florida. The Golden Knights led 24-20 late in the third quarter when the Gamecocks got the gift that they ultimately turned into a neatly wrapped victory.

With 1:27 left in the third, the Knights fumbled, and practically everybody in uniform went for the ball. Atkins was on the bottom of a huge pileup, digging, grabbing, and clawing for the ball with everybody else. The refs said he had it. Never mind that Atkins said he didn't (not to the refs, of course).

"To be honest, that was a gift," Atkins said. "It was a blitz, and I went for the ball and got on it, but the ball slid out from under me, and the Central Florida dude recovered." But why did an official signal Gamecock ball? "I guess since I was the first one to the ball, the referees went ahead and gave it to me," Atkins said. "They gave us a gift, which I'm not going to argue with."

Especially since that gift was the turning point in the game. Gaining possession at the Central Florida 43, USC used eight plays to score and take the lead for good at 27-24. The Gamecocks won 33-31.

"I guess it turned out to be a pretty big play," Atkins said in an understatement. "Sometimes you have to be lucky too, and I guess we were on that play." And a gift or two along the way doesn't hurt either.

Receiving a gift – such as a favorable call from the officials – is quite nice, but giving has its pleasures too, doesn't it? The children's excitement on Christmas morning. Your spouse's smile of sheer delight for that really cool anniversary present. Your dad's surprise that time you didn't give him a tie or socks. There really does seem to be something to this being more blessed to give than to receive.

No matter how generous we may be, though, we are grumbling misers compared to God, who is the greatest gift-giver of all. That's because all the good things in our lives – every one of them – come from God. Friends, love, health, family, the air we breathe, the sun that warms us, even our very lives are all gifts from a profligate God. And here's the kicker: He even gives us eternal life with him through the gift of his son.

What in the world can we possibly give God in return? Our love and our life.

From what we get, we can make a living; what we give, however, makes a life.

– Arthur Ashe

Nobody can match God when it comes to giving, but you can give him the gift of your love in appreciation.

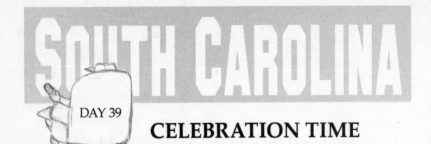

DAY 39

CELEBRATION TIME

Read Exodus 14:26-31; 15:19-21.

"Miriam the prophetess, Aaron's sister, took a tambourine in her hand, and all the women followed her, with tambourines and dancing" (v. 15:20).

South Carolina celebrated twice, Ohio State once. Fortunately, USC's second celebration came last in the most thrilling Gamecock bowl game ever.

The 2002 Outback Bowl between South Carolina and Ohio State was a blowout. Behind Phil Petty's pinpoint passing and two touchdown runs from Andrew Pinnock, the Gamecocks led 28-0 in the third quarter. As writer Michael Smith put it, at that point "the Gamecocks apparently started thinking about [their] victory celebration." That is, they quit playing ball and started celebrating. Nobody bothered to tell the Buckeyes, however, that the game was over.

As the Gamecock faithful watched in dismay, Ohio State scored on the last play of the third quarter and then rolled up more than 200 passing yards in the fourth quarter and tied the game at 28. The situation got worse when Petty, who was the game MVP with 227 yards passing and two touchdowns, made a rare mistake and tossed an interception with only 1:12 to play.

That's when the Buckeyes threw a premature victory celebration of their own. They drew a 15-yard excessive celebration penalty that backed them up to their own 18. Instead of playing for overtime, the Buckeyes tried to catch the Gamecocks napping with a long pass. Cornerback Sheldon Brown intercepted and returned it 37 yards to the Ohio State 29. On the game's final play, Daniel Weaver kicked a 42-yard field goal for the 31-28 win.

The real celebration began. USC's players rushed Weaver and buried him in a pile. The underclassmen then gave the thirteen seniors who had led the team to 17 wins in two seasons – the best run in school history – a celebratory ride around the field.

You know what it takes to throw a good party. You start with your closest friends, add some salsa and chips, fire up the grill and throw on some burgers and dogs, and then top it all off with the South Carolina game on TV.

You probably also know that any old excuse will do to get people together for a celebration. All you really need is a sense that life is pretty good right now.

That's the thing about having Jesus as part of your life: He turns every day into a celebration of the good life. No matter what tragedies or setbacks life may have in store, the heart given to Jesus will find the joy in living. That's because such a life is spent with quiet confidence in God's promise of salvation through Jesus, a confidence that inevitably bubbles up into a joy the troubles of the world cannot touch. When a life is celebrated with Jesus, the party never stops.

Aim high and celebrate that!

> *– Marathon runner Bill Rodgers*

**With Jesus, life is one big party
because it becomes a celebration of victory and joy.**

DAY 40

AMAZING!

Read: Luke 4:31-36.

"All the people were amazed and said to each other, "What is this teaching? With authority and power he gives orders to evil spirits and they come out!"" (v. 36)

One of the most amazing shots in Gamecock basketball history completed one of the most amazing comebacks in any sport.

Eddie Fogler's men's team of 1997-98 was one of the best in South Carolina history. They finished 23-8 and made it to the NCAA Tournament. On Feb. 1, though, against Cincinnati and with a national TV audience watching, they didn't look like much. They trailed 39-19 at halftime and 42-19 as the last half began.

The players didn't quit, though, and gradually they whittled the Cincinnati lead to single digits.

South Carolina trailed 65-59 with 2:43 left. Melvin Watson hit three free throws and a jump shot to make it 65-64 with 44 seconds left. Cincinnati seemed to have withstood the South Carolina assault with a steal with only 12 seconds left, but the Gamecocks got one last shot when freshman Antonio Grant drew a charge with only 5.2 seconds left. The stage was set for an amazing finish.

The Gamecocks hurried the ball into the frontcourt and called time out with 4.1 seconds left on the clock. They then inbounded the ball to B.J. McKie, their leading scorer, but Cincinnati was ready. The Bearcats immediately double-teamed him. Losing his balance and on the verge of falling down, McKie managed to punch the ball to midcourt where Grant grabbed the loose ball and let fly with a 25-footer just before the buzzer screamed. The wing and a prayer found the net for an amazing 67-65 Gamecock win that featured a comeback from a 23-point deficit.

The word *amazing* defines the limits of what you believe to be plausible or usual. The Grand Canyon, the birth of your children, those last-second South Carolina wins after being way behind -- they're amazing! You've never seen anything like that before!

Some people in Galilee felt the same way when they encountered Jesus. Jesus amazed them with the authority of his teaching, and he wowed them with his power over spirit beings. People everywhere just couldn't quit talking about him.

It would have been amazing had they not been amazed. They were, after all, witnesses to the most amazing spectacle in the history of the world: God himself was right there among them walking, talking, teaching, preaching, and healing.

Their amazement should be a part of your life too because Jesus still lives. The almighty and omnipotent God of the universe seeks to spend time with you every day – because he loves you. Amazing!

It's amazing. Some of the greatest characteristics of being a winning football player are the same ones found in a Christian man.
-- Bobby Bowden

Everything about God is amazing,
but perhaps most amazing of all is that
he loves us and desires our company.

THE REWARD

Read 1 Corinthians 3:10-17.

"If what he has built survives, he will receive his reward"
(v. 14).

On the flight home, Billy DuPre got an unusual and quite enjoyable reward for his game-winning kick against Virginia Tech in 1969.

With such stars as quarterback Tommy Suggs, running back Warren Muir, and two-time All-ACC receiver Fred Zeigler, Paul Dietzel's Gamecocks won their only ACC championship that season, going undefeated in conference play. In the game against Virginia Tech, though, the Hokies scored on a 26-yard touchdown pass to lead 16-14 with only 1:13 left.

DuPre (1968-70) was South Carolina's first soccer-style place-kicker, and at only 5-5 and 150 pounds, probably the smallest. On Oct. 18, however, he stood among the giants. After the Tech kickoff, Suggs moved the Gamecocks to the Hokie 29 with only nine seconds left. DuPre had missed two earlier attempts, but he nailed this one, a 47-yarder that tied the school record for the longest field goal. South Carolina won 17-16.

In the press box, assistant coach Don "Scooter" Purvis hyper-ventilated from the excitement and passed out. He recovered by the time he reached a hospital, but Dietzel decided to make some switches in the flights home to allow Purvis to fly in the athletic department's twin-engine Cessna. That meant the charter flight had 96 passengers and room for only 95. An airline representative solved the problem by suggesting that the smallest person could sit in one of the flight attendant's jump seats.

That smallest person, of course, was DuPre, who thus suffered the indignity of flying home while strapped in a folding jump seat. He didn't mind one bit, however. The whole trip he was surrounded by and fussed over by the charter's working flight attendants, described as "two very attractive young ladies."

We want our rewards now. Hire a new football coach; he better win right away. You want to keep me happy? Then let's see a raise and a promotion immediately or I'm looking for another job. Want that new car or big house you can't afford? Hey that's what they make credit for, so I can live the good life without having to wait.

Jesus spoke often about rewards, but in terms of eternal salvation and service to others rather than instant gratification or self-aggrandizement. The reward that Jesus has in mind for us is the inevitable result of the way of life he taught. To live with faith in God and in service to others is to move surely – if not swiftly – toward the eternal rewards included in our salvation.

The world's ephemeral material rewards may well pass us by if we don't grab them right now. God's eternal spiritual rewards, however, will be ours.

The price of victory is high but so are the rewards.

-- *Bear Bryant*

**God rewards our faith, patience, and service
by fulfilling the promises he has made to us.**

DAY 42

CALLING IT QUITS

Read Numbers 13:25-14:4.

"The men who had gone up with him said, 'We can't attack those people; they are stronger than we are'" (v. 13:31).

Mike Hold told his dad he was quitting USC football. That was right before he quarterbacked the Gamecocks to their greatest season ever.

Hold planned to walk on at Arizona State after junior college until Joe Morrison offered him a scholarship. He arrived in Columbia in 1983 with Arizona still on his mind. "I made two Ds and a B my first semester," he said. "I was trying to get out so bad." After the semester break, though, he "kind of settled in and started making friends."

Hold was redshirted in 1983 and began 1984 as the backup to Allen Mitchell. By his own admission Hold was "a loosey-goosey type of guy. You know, kind of a California guy," and offensive coordinator Frank Sadler didn't like it. He even told Hold, "As long as I'm offensive coordinator you will never play here." That's when Hold called his dad and announced he was coming home. His dad said he could, but asked his son to do one thing that Gamecock fans are grateful for to this day: "Stay one more week. You're in practice; you owe it to the team to at least do that."

The next game was against 12th-ranked Georgia. Mitchell got hurt in the third quarter; Hold came in and led the team to a

GAMECOCKS

17-10 upset. He had a 66-yard quick kick and a 62-yard pass to Ira Hillary that set up the game-winning touchdown, which he scored on a two-yard run.

The Gamecocks were on their way to a 10-1 season. Hold left USC with the third highest number of passing yards in school history. He later said that coming to South Carolina "was the best decision I've ever made in my life."

Listening to his dad and not quitting was a close second.

Remember that time you quit a high-school sports team? Bailed out of a relationship? Walked away from that job with the goals unachieved? Sometimes quitting is the most sensible way to minimize your losses, so you may well at times in your life give up on something or someone.

In your relationship with God, however, you should remember the people of Israel, who quit when the Promised Land was theirs for the taking. They forgot one fact of life you never should: God never gives up on you. That means you should never, ever give up on God. No matter how tired or discouraged you get, no matter that it seems your prayers aren't getting through to God, no matter what – quitting on God is not an option. He is preparing a blessing for you, and in his time, he will bring it to fruition -- if you don't quit on him.

The first time you quit, it's hard. The second time, it gets easier. The third time, you don't even have to think about it.
-- Bear Bryant

Whatever else you give up on in your life, don't give up on God; he will never ever give up on you.

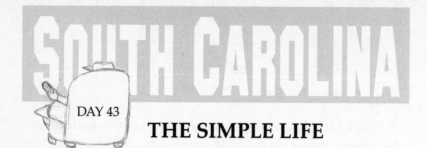
DAY 43

THE SIMPLE LIFE

Read 1 John 1:5-10.

"If we confess our sins, he is faithful and just and will forgive us our sins and purify us from all unrighteousness" (v. 9).

Work hard. Stay in shape.

It's so simple it's ridiculous. But those simple instructions jumpstarted the 1993 men's soccer team to the greatest season in Gamecock history.

In the spring, head coach Mark Berson realized that he had the talent on hand for a landmark season in the fall, so he came up with a winning formula. Berson told his plays to do two things: work hard and return in the fall in good shape. That was it.

The players believed him. "Coach told us last spring that it was there for us if we wanted it bad enough," said senior midfielder/ forward Matt Haiduk. "Believe it or not, we really did believe we were capable of something like this."

So what was "this"? It wasn't the 16-4-4 overall record, the Metro Conference championship, or the longest win streak ever that made the season so sensational. After all, the Gamecocks had kicked their way to winning seasons ever since Berson became the program's first head coach in 1978. As one writer put it, "Berson didn't inherit a winning tradition; he created one."

What made this season special was what the Gamecocks did once the regular season was over. They advanced all the way to the NCAA championship game for the first time in school history. In the semifinals, midfielder/defender Jamie Posnanski scored from five yards out for the game's only goal and a win over Cal State-Fullerton.

The Gamecocks lost to Virginia in the championship game, but the team had added its name to USC lore – partly because their coach had a simple formula and they stuck to it.

Perhaps the simple life in America was doomed by the arrival of the programmable VCR. Since then, we've been on an inevitably downward spiral into ever more complicated lives. Even windshield wipers have multiple settings now, and figuring out a clothes dryer requires a graduate degree.

But you might do well in your own life to mimic the simple formula Mark Berson had for his team. That is, you should approach your life with the keen awareness that success requires simplicity, a sticking to the basics: Revere God, love your family, honor your country, do your best.

Theologians may make what God did in Jesus as complicated as quantum mechanics and the infield fly rule, but God kept it simple for you: believe, trust, and obey. Believe in Jesus as the Son of God, trust that through him God makes possible your deliverance from your sins into Heaven, and obey God in the way he wants you to live. It's simple, but it's the true winning formula.

I think God made it simple. Just accept Him and believe.
-- Bobby Bowden

Life continues to get more complicated, but God made it simple for us when he showed up as Jesus.

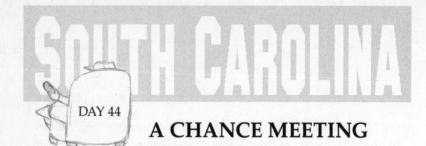

DAY 44

A CHANCE MEETING

Read Luke 24:13-35.

*"That same day two of them were going to a village. . . .
They were talking with each other about everything that
had happened. . . . Jesus himself came up and walked
along with them" (vv. 13-15).*

A chance encounter changed Dominic Fusci's life forever.

Fusci grew up in Greenwich Village in the 1930s and '40s and had an appointment with a coach from the Naval Academy during a coaching convention at a hotel. When he walked in, reporters were gathered around South Carolina Coach Rex Enright. To Fusci's surprise, one of the reporters said, "Here comes the kid now." Enright approached him, and the kid from New York was soon on a bus to Columbia. Fusci started for three seasons on both sides of the line, his play interrupted by World War II. He was inducted into the USC Athletic Hall of Fame in 1993.

In his first game against Tennessee in 1942, Fusci discovered his Southern teammates were chewing tobacco. He'd never tried it, but he took a big chaw and was okay with it until he was nailed on the kickoff and swallowed the plug. He was immediately ghastly ill and hit the huddle moaning. His unsympathetic teammates chased him away because they couldn't hear the play call.

When Fusci lined up groaning, hacking, coughing, and foaming, one dismayed Tennessee player said, 'Hey, this guy is having a heart attack." Center Lou Sossamon, who that season became

GAMECOCKS

USC's first All-America, replied, "Nah. He's been acting like that ever since that dog bit him on Monday." Needless to say, the Volunteers gave Fusci a wide berth until he managed to cough up the tobacco and feel better.

After that inauspicious beginning, Fusci starred for the Gamecocks and stayed in South Carolina after graduation, his life forever changed by a chance meeting in a New York hotel.

Maybe you met your spouse on a blind date or in Kroger's frozen food section. Perhaps a conversation in an elevator or over lunch led to a job offer. Chance meetings – even those in hotel lobbies -- often shape our lives. Some meetings, however, are too important to be left to what seem like the whims of life. If your child is sick, you don't wait until you happen to bump into a physician at Starbuck's to seek help.

So it is with Jesus. Too much is at stake to leave a meeting with him to chance. Instead, you intentionally seek him at church, in the pages of your Bible, on your knees in prayer, or through a conversation with a friend or neighbor. How you conduct the search doesn't matter; what matters is that you find him.

Once you've met Jesus, the acquaintance should then be intentionally cultivated until it is a deep, abiding, life-shaping and life-changing friendship.

If you think it's hard to meet new people, try picking up the wrong golf ball.

-- Jack Lemmon

A meeting with Jesus should not be a chance encounter, but instead should be sought out.

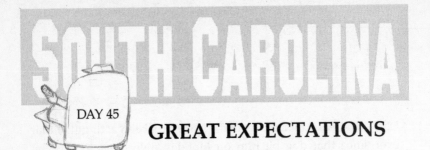

DAY 45

GREAT EXPECTATIONS

Read John 1:43-51.

"'Nazareth! Can anything good come from there?'
Nathanael asked" (v. 46).

Because he raised expectations in Columbia to such unprecedented heights, Paul Dietzel probably had himself to blame most of all for his demise.

Dietzel arrived at USC in the spring of 1966, bringing with him an immediate level of excitement. In 1969, the Gamecocks went 7-3, won their first and only ACC championship, and received what was called their first "bonafide" invitation to a bowl game. While that success ratcheted expectations up a notch, a project and a decision that Dietzel championed ultimately created expectations he couldn't match.

The project was the expansion and renaming of Carolina Stadium. Dietzel's excellence as a promoter and fundraiser was on display for every fan to see when the Gamecocks opened the 1971 season in what was now known as Williams-Brice Stadium, 55,000 seats strong. The decision was to leave the ACC after the 1969 season. Dietzel argued that because of the limitations the conference put on recruiting, only as an independent could South Carolina become a national football power.

As one writer put it, "Dietzel had only himself to blame for the rise in expectations." *The State* wrote, "All those loyal people who have jammed the stadium week after week and have contributed heavily to fund-raising programs are soon going to be expecting, and justly so, something more than just thrills and moral victories." Those expectations weren't met, however.

The Gamecocks went 4-6-1 in 1970, 6-5 in 1971, and 4-7 in 1972. A 7-4 1973 season behind quarterback Jeff Grantz relieved some of the pressure, but two games into the 4-7 season of 1974, Dietzel resigned as head coach effective at season's end.

The blind date your friend promised would look like Brad Pitt or Jennifer Aniston but resembled a Munster. Your vacation that went downhill after the lost luggage. The promise offered by a new head football coach. Often your expectations are raised only to be dashed. Sometimes it's best not to get your hopes up; then at least you have the possibility of being surprised.

Worst of all, perhaps, is when you realize that you are the one not meeting others' expectations. The fact is, though, that you aren't here to live up to what others think of you. Jesus didn't; in part, that's why they killed him. But he did meet God's expectations for his life, which was all that really mattered.

Because God's kingdom is so great, God does have great expectations for any who would enter, and you should not take them lightly. What the world expects from you is of no importance; what God expects from you is paramount.

You live up -- or down -- to your expectations.
-- Lou Holtz

You have little if anything to gain from meeting the world's expectations of you; you have all of eternity to gain from meeting God's.

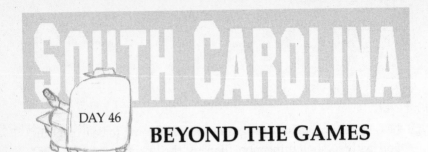

DAY 46

BEYOND THE GAMES

Read Galatians 5:16-26.

*"So I say, live by the Spirit. . . . The sinful nature desires
what is contrary to the Spirit. . . . The acts of the sinful
nature are obvious: . . . I warn you, as I did before, that
those who live like this will not inherit the kingdom of
God" (vv. 16, 17, 19, 21).*

The cold, hard statistics say he was not a success at South Carolina. Shawn Valdes-Fauli knew otherwise.

Twelve appearances in 2006 totaling 11.1 innings with one win and three saves. That's it in the Gamecock record books.

But Valdes-Fauli's appearance in the opening game of the 2006 season against Elon on Feb. 10 was a testimony to courage and persistence. "I've been working 26 years with student-athletes, and I try to . . . find an understanding of what they are going through," said USC baseball coach Ray Tanner. "But I can't, for the life of me, begin to understand what Shawn has gone through."

Valdes-Fauli pitched successfully for the Miami Hurricanes in 2002 and 2003. In October 2002, though, his brother committed suicide; guilt and grief weighed heavily on the younger brother. He missed classes, his grades slipped, and he eventually was kicked off the team.

At the urging of a Miami coach, Tanner gave Valdes-Fauli a second chance. During his first pitching session as a Gamecock, Valdes-Fauli blew out his elbow. He underwent Tommy John surgery and a year of rehabilitation. A concerned Tanner told Shawn's parents their son might be better off closer to home.

But Valdes-Fauli stayed in Columbia. He worked his arm and his grades back into shape, even making the dean's list. When he took the mound against Elon, Valdes-Fauli swiped his brother's initials in the dirt. He then retired all eight batters he faced and got the win. Shawn Valdes-Fauli was a winner.

Are you a successful person? Your answer, of course, depends upon how you define success. Is the measure of your success based on the number of digits in your bank balance, the square footage of your house, or that title on your office door?

Certainly the world determines success by wealth, fame, prestige, awards, and possessions. Our culture screams that life is all about gratifying your own needs and wants. If it feels good, do it. It's basically the Beach Boys' philosophy of life.

But all success of this type has one glaring shortcoming: You can't take it with you. Eventually, Daddy takes the T-bird away. Like life itself, all these things are fleeting.

A more lasting way to approach success is through the spiritual rather than the physical. The goal becomes not money or backslaps by sycophants but eternal life spent with God. Success of that kind is forever.

Success demands singleness of purpose.

-- Vince Lombardi

**Success isn't permanent and failure isn't fatal
unless you're talking about
your relationship with God.**

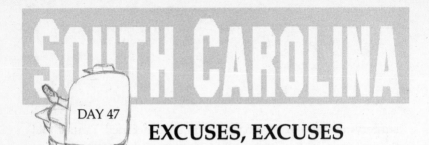

DAY 47

EXCUSES, EXCUSES

Read Luke 9:57-62.

"Another said, 'I will follow you, Lord; but first let me go back and say good-by to my family'" (v. 61).

Exhaustion and oysters were the excuses for a loss the South Carolina football team suffered in 1896.

It was a pivotal year in the history of USC football. "Aware that football was the latest phenomenon in athletics and outraged that the SCC [South Carolina College] administration was not taking steps to remain competitive," the students shouted so loudly and so insistently that the school hired its first football coach, W.H. "Dixie" Whaley. Perhaps the discomfiting news from up the road that Clemson had hired a football coach helped goad the administration into action.

On Nov. 12, 1896, Big Thursday was born. South Carolina's first-ever touchdown against Clemson was scored by N.W. Brooker. Cantzon Foster's 15-yard run in the last half proved to be the difference. Team captain C.H. McLaurin kicked both extra points as South Carolina's Jaguars won 12-6.

After that, though, came a loss to Wofford and a season-ending 12-0 defeat by Furman on Nov. 26. Whaley said several factors played into the loss to Furman. First of all, the team did not leave for Greenville until 8 a.m. Saturday and then spent six hours on the train. Once they arrived, the "ravenous" Jaguars wolfed down a pregame meal of raw oysters. They then suited up and rode by horse and wagon the two miles to the field. They arrived, "totally exhausted," according to Whaley, about five minutes before kickoff. "By that time," the head coach lamented, "the boys were beginning to feel a little green around the gills from their oyster luncheon." Whaley, who left coaching after the season to begin his successful law practice, called it a "miracle" that the boys could play at all.

Has some of your most creative thinking involved excuses for not going in to work? Have you discovered that an unintended benefit of computers is that you can always blame them for the destruction of all your hard work? Don't you manage to stammer or stutter some justification when a state trooper pulls you over? We're usually pretty good at making excuses – maybe even oysters and exhaustion -- to cover our failures or to get out of something we don't particularly want to do.

That holds true for our faith life also. The Bible is too hard to understand so I won't read it; the weather's too pretty to be shut up in church; praying in public is embarrassing and I'm not very good at it anyway. The plain truth is, though, that whatever excuses we make for not following Jesus wholeheartedly are not good enough.

Jesus made no excuses to avoid dying for us; we should offer none to avoid living for him.

There are a thousand reasons for failure but not a single excuse.
-- Former NFL player Mike Reid

Try though we might, no excuses can justify
our failure to follow Jesus wholeheartedly.

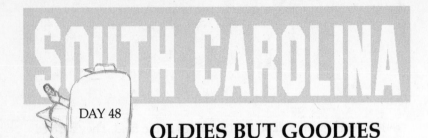
DAY 48

OLDIES BUT GOODIES

Read Psalm 92.

"[The righteous] will still bear fruit in old age, they will stay fresh and green, proclaiming, 'The Lord is upright'" (vv. 14-15).

Pops. That nickname his Carolina teammates gave him says it all. Tim "Pops" Frisby may well be the oldest man ever to play major college football, at least in the modern age.

In 2004, Frisby was one of sixty walk-ons trying to make the Gamecock team. A trim and fit wide receiver, he drew little notice until rumors began to surface. Finally, his skeptical teammates confronted him: Was he really almost 40 years old? In reply, Frisby pulled out his driver's license; the math revealed he was 39.

Frisby was the father of six, a 20-year Army veteran and former Ranger who served in the first Gulf War and in Kosovo. He made the team, and when the NCAA Clearinghouse – which was not in existence when Frisby graduated from high school – certified his eligibility to play, he became a national celebrity. He was aware of the hoopla surrounding him (He appeared on *Late Night with David Letterman.*), but both Coach Lou Holtz and he insisted he was on the team because he could contribute. "He's going to play this year because he deserves to play," Holtz said. "The last thing I want to be is a novelty," Frisby said. "I just wanted to play football and fulfill a dream."

On the Saturday night following his clearance, he got in on

the last four plays against Troy. His job was to block, but the Troy cornerback played so far off him, he never made contact.

He got into the Clemson game that season, and then in 2005, at the age of 40, the old man of college football caught a pass against Troy, fulfilling a promise Steve Spurrier had made before the season began. After the season, Frisby retired, though he did graduate from USC *cum laude*.

Thirty-nine is a rather advanced age to start a football career, but in our youth-obsessed culture, we usually don't like to admit – even to ourselves – that we're not as young as we used to be no matter how old we are.

So we keep plastic surgeons in business, dye our hair, buy cases of those miracle wrinkle-reducing creams, and redouble our efforts in the gym. Sometimes, though, we just have to face up to the truth the mirror tells us: We're getting older every day.

It's really all right, though, because aging and old age are part of the natural cycle of our lives, which was God's idea in the first place. God's conception of the golden years, though, doesn't include unlimited close encounters with a rocking chair and nothing more. God expects us to serve him as we are able all the days of our life. Those who serve God flourish no matter their age because the energizing power of God is in them.

Age is a question of mind over matter. If you don't mind, it doesn't matter.

-- *Pitcher and philosopher Satchel Paige*

Servants of God don't ever retire; they keep working until they get the ultimate promotion.

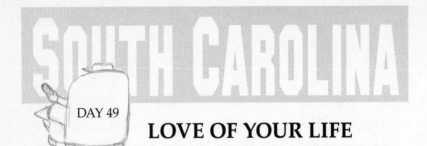

SOUTH CAROLINA

DAY 49

LOVE OF YOUR LIFE

Read 1 John 4:7-21.

"Whoever does not love does not know God, because God is love" (v. 8).

Love conquers all, but sometimes soccer can help.

At a summer camp for local soccer players in Vermont, Jamie Smith first laid eyes on a counselor named Shelley Addison. She was a rising junior at the University of Vermont and a center midfielder for the college soccer team. He was a rising sophomore at Providence College and a goalkeeper on the college team. His first thought was how attractive she was; his second thought was that she was a good player. She thought he was funny.

On the final night of camp at a party for the counselors, they finally got a chance to talk and to know each other. Soccer had brought them together, but it would also drag them 265 miles apart to their respective schools. Shelley was hesitant about a long-distance relationship, but Jamie persisted.

They married in 1996, but soccer separated them again when Shelley became the head women's soccer coach at the University of Rhode Island while Jamie was on the staff at Dartmouth.

When Shelley led the Rams to a 15-4-1 record in her fourth season, athletic directors took notice. One of them was Mike McGee, who was scrambling to replace Sue Kelly, who had resigned as women's soccer coach at USC. The Smiths insisted they come as a pair with Shelley the head coach. Uncertain about a husband

and wife team, McGee wanted to meet Jamie. "Although she is very capable, I'd have a very difficult time working for my wife," he said. Jamie has no such problem. As Shelley told McGee, "You can't get a more loyal assistant than your husband."

Thus, in 2001, the Smiths came to Columbia. Love – and soccer -- had brought them together again.

Your heart rate accelerates, your blood pressure jumps, your mouth runs dry, your vision blurs, and you start stammering. Either you've got the flu or the one you're in love with just walked into the room and smiled at you. Fortunately, if the attraction is based on more than hormones and eye candy, the feverish frenzy that characterizes newfound love matures into a deeper, more meaningful affection. If it didn't, we'd probably die from exhaustion, stroke, heart failure, or a combination thereof.

We pursue true love with a desperation and a ferocity that is unmatched by any other desire. Ultimately, the Christian life is about that same search, about falling in love and becoming a partner in a deep-seated, satisfying, ever-growing and ever-deepening relationship. The Christian life is about loving so fiercely and so completely that love is not something you're in but something you are. The object of your love is the greatest and most faithful lover of them all: God.

Most people have a harder time letting themselves love than finding someone to love them.

– NBA Hall-of-Famer Bill Russell

God is head-over-heels in love with you;
like any lover, he wants you to return the love.

DAY 50

THE BIG TIME

Read Matthew 2:19-23.

"He went and lived in a town called Nazareth" (v. 23).

From the rural Georgia countryside to the Super Bowl, Dan Reeves made the long trip from the backwoods to the big time.

Reeves attended Americus High School in South Georgia, but he wasn't really from town. Rather, he grew up on a farm about six miles out in the country. He was a two-sport star, and when South Carolina came calling, he was on his way.

Reeves arrived in Columbia in 1961, and the country boy had an immediate communication problem because all his backfield mates were from the North. "They couldn't understand me, and I couldn't understand them for about the first two weeks," he recalled. As an 18-year-old sophomore in 1962, Reeves became the youngest starting quarterback in the nation. Before he finished, he was USC's all-time leading passer with 2,561 yards and 16 touchdowns.

Nevertheless, Reeves considered himself a running quarterback who "could throw halfway decent," so he didn't expect the NFL to be very interested in him. But the Dallas Cowboys were, and he moved onto a bigger stage for an eight-year career.

His playing days over, Reeves figured his days in the spotlight were over too. He went into the real estate business until he got a chance to return to the NFL as an assistant coach. Then in 1981 he hit the big time for real: head coach of the Denver Broncos.

GAMECOCKS

As head honcho of the Broncos, New York Giants, and Atlanta Falcons, Reeves strode across the biggest stage the sports world has to offer. In his career as a player, assistant coach, and head coach, he went to the Super Bowl nine times.

He traveled a long way from that farm in South Georgia.

The move to the big time is one we often desire to make in our own lives. Bumps in the road, one stoplight communities, and towns with only a service station, a church, and a voting place litter the American countryside. Maybe you were born in one of them and grew up in a virtually unknown village in a backwater county. Perhaps you started out on a stage far removed from the bright lights of Broadway, the glitz of Hollywood, or the halls of power in Washington, D.C.

Those original circumstances don't have to define or limit you, though, for life is much more than geography. It is about character and walking with God whether you're in the countryside or the city.

Jesus knew the truth of that. After all, he grew up in a small town in an inconsequential region of an insignificant country ruled by foreign invaders.

Where you are doesn't matter. What you are does.

I live so far out in the country that I have to walk toward town to go hunting.
-- Former Major Leaguer Rocky Bridges

**Where you live may largely be
the culmination of a series of circumstances;
what you are is a choice you make.**

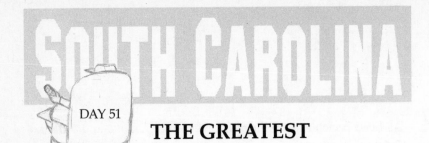
DAY 51

THE GREATEST

Read Mark 9:33-37.

"If anyone wants to be first, he must be the very last, and the servant of all" (v. 35).

The readers of *The State* in 2004 named Jeff Grantz as the greatest quarterback in South Carolina history.

Grantz led the Gamecocks to winning seasons in 1973 and in 1975 and was 2-1 against Clemson. The 1975 team went to the Tangerine Bowl. In 1985, Grantz was inducted into the University of South Carolina Athletic Hall of Fame. The state hall of fame followed in 1988.

Grantz benefitted from Coach Paul Dietzel's decision before the 1973 season to switch to the veer offense. Grantz was made for it. "South Carolina's offensive line knew how to block, and Grantz knew how to read it." The Gamecocks went 7-4 behind Grantz in 1973 but fell to 4-7 in 1974, and Jim Carlen replaced Dietzel.

Grantz saved his best for the last home game of his career, Clemson in 1975. He rushed for 122 yards and a touchdown and passed for five touchdowns. The offense rolled up 616 yards and humiliated the Tigers 56-20. Clarence Williams needed 113 yards rushing to pass 1,000 for the season, and he romped for 160 including a 36-yard touchdown run on the Gamecocks' first possession.

Clemson was never in the game. South Carolina led 35-6 at halftime and 49-12 in the third quarter. The Gamecocks never had to punt, scoring on nine straight possessions, though one touchdown was nullified by a penalty.

"We just rolled that day, in control from start to finish," Grantz said. "It was a great win for us and it was the end of a great, fun career."

And it was a fitting end to the playing days of the quarterback fans voted South Carolina's greatest ever.

We all want to be the greatest. For instance, the goal for the Gamecocks and their fans every season is the conference championship and a major bowl. The competition at work is to be the most productive sales person on the staff or the Teacher of the Year. In other words, we define being the greatest in terms of the struggle for personal success. It's nothing new; Jesus' disciples saw greatness in the same way.

As Jesus illustrated, though, greatness in the Kingdom of God has nothing to do with the world's understanding of success. Rather, the greatest are those who channel their ambition toward the furtherance of Christ's kingdom through love and service, rather than their own advancement, which is a complete reversal of status and values as the world sees them.

After all, who could be greater than the person who has Jesus for a brother and God for a father? And that's every one of us.

My goal was to be the greatest athlete that ever lived.
                                            -- Babe Didrikson Zaharias

**To be great for God has nothing to do
with personal advancement and everything to do
with the advancement of Christ's kingdom.**

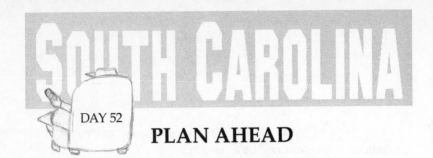
DAY 52

PLAN AHEAD

Read Psalm 33:1-15.

"The plans of the Lord stand firm forever, the purposes of his heart through all generations" (v. 11).

The Mongoose. For South Carolina men's basketball coach Chuck Noe, it was an offense he devised to offset the superior talent of other teams.

Noe came to Columbia in 1962. He looked around and saw that he was using the likes of 6-4 Bob Haney and 6-6 John Schroeder at center against players who were 6-8 or 7-0. The Mongoose thus became a matter of survival, and since the shot clock wasn't in play then, the strategy worked quite well.

Moe would station three players at mid-court, the center in the middle and his two best ball handlers on either side. They would hold the ball as long as the defenders didn't come out and apply pressure. If the defense got bored, one of the two players near the baseline would break for the basket, take a pass, and score.

Moe used the Mongoose to whip Furman in 1963. The Game-cocks led 19-17 at halftime with Ronnie Collins scoring all but two of USC's points.

Noe was not averse to using unusual strategies to gain an edge. When nationally ranked Duke came to town, Noe stationed the pep band directly behind the Duke bench. The band was so close that the trombone player's instrument kept sliding past the Duke coach's ear. He finally took his team to mid-court during timeouts to escape the din.

Noe once told center Jim Fox that before a game he should eat a lot of garlic and breathe on the opposing center.

Exhaustion forced the intense Noe to resign midway through his second season in Columbia, but he apparently never tired of planning ahead to get any edge he could for his team.

Successful living – just like successful coaching -- takes planning. You go to school to improve your chances for a better paying job. You use blueprints to build your home. You plan for retirement. You map out your vacation to have the best time. You even plan your children -- sometimes.

Your best-laid plans, however, sometime get wrecked by events and circumstances beyond your control. The economy goes into the tank; a debilitating illness strikes; a hurricane hits. Life is capricious and thus no plans -- not even your best ones -- are foolproof.

But you don't have to go it alone. God has plans for your life that guarantee success as God defines it if you will make him your planning partner. God's plan for your life includes joy, love, peace, kindness, gentleness, and faithfulness, all the elements necessary for truly successful living for today and for all eternity. And God's plan will not fail.

If you don't know where you are going, you will wind up somewhere else.

-- *Yogi Berra*

Your plans help ensure a successful life; God's plans absolutely ensure a successful eternity.

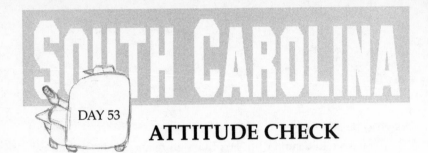

DAY 53

ATTITUDE CHECK

Read 1 Thessalonians 5.

"Give thanks in all circumstances, for this is God's will for you in Christ Jesus" (v. 18).

He was a good player but he had a bad attitude."

That's exactly how Dunta Robinson said he didn't want to be remembered, but when he came to Columbia in 2000, that's exactly how he could have been characterized. For instance, he was convinced he wouldn't make any friends at South Carolina. "I just remember thinking, 'I don't think I'm going to make a lot of close friends here,'" Robinson recalled.

He also expected to play immediately. "I didn't care about anything. I just wanted to be on the field," Robinson said. "That was my first thing: Just play, no matter what." There were two problems with that attitude: Corners Andre Goodman and Sheldon Brown – both of whom were drafted by the NFL in 2002 – were ahead of him

So here was a guy who expected that he would never get to play very much and who also didn't think he'd make any friends. "I was wrong," Robinson said. On both counts.

Robinson matured into one of the most likeable guys on the team, and when he did get a chance to play as a junior corner in 2002, he led the Gamecocks with four interceptions and ten pass breakups. His senior season, he was voted a team captain, was the Defensive Most Valuable Player, and was the tenth player taken in the NFL draft. "He's a cool cat to be around," cornerback Teddy Crawford said of Robinson. He was, according to Crawford, "what a captain's supposed to be."

"I just want people to remember me as that guy who went out there and gave it all he had," Robinson said. "Just somebody who made his teammates better and somebody that people can get along with." And not somebody with a bad attitude.

How's your attitude? You can fuss because your house is not as big as some, because a coworker talks too much, or because you have to take pills every day. Or you can appreciate your home for providing warmth and shelter, the co-worker for the lively conversation, and the medicine for keeping you reasonably healthy.

Whether life is endured or enjoyed depends largely on your attitude. An attitude of thankfulness to God offers you the best chance to get the most out of your life because living in gratitude means you choose joy in your life no matter what your circumstances. This world does not exist to satisfy you, so chances are it will not. True contentment and joy are found in a deep, abiding relationship with God, and the proper way to approach God is not with haughtiness or anger but with gratitude for all he has given you.

I became an optimist when I discovered that I wasn't going to win any more games by being anything else.
-- Former major league manager Earl Weaver

Your attitude goes a long way
toward determining the quality of your life
and your relationship with God.

DAY 54

POWER PLAY

Read Psalm 28.

"The Lord is my strength and my shield; my heart trusts in him, and I am helped" (v. 7a).

Alex Hawkins said Jake Bodkin was the strongest man he ever knew. He was also one of the greatest linemen – and one of the most original characters -- in South Carolina football history.

Bodkin, who died in 2007, was an All-ACC guard and team captain in 1960, his senior season. He roomed with Hawkins in Columbia; they had played together in high school when Hawkins was the quarterback and Bodkin was his center. Bodkin went into the service after graduation, and when he got out, as Hawkins put it, "I got him a scholarship. I figured they owed me something since they weren't paying me."

Thus, Bodkin became Hawkins' "constant cohort for campus shenanigans." Armed with a 1927 Rio, the pair had a chauffeur's outfit that Libby (Hawkins' college sweetheart and later his wife) would don and then drive them around campus and town. Bodkin usually cranked the car -- without any trouble -- but one time Hawkins tried it and promptly broke his toe when he put his foot in the wrong place. Hawkins sheepishly faced Coach Warren Giese before practice and told him how he had suffered his injury. Giese in turn told Hawkins two things: 1) he would play that weekend despite the broken toe; and 2) he should never imitate Bodkin in anything "because Bodkin wasn't like other people."

GAMECOCKS

Which was certainly true. Bodkin would stick a pin through his neck, his lips, or his legs to win bets and spending money. When everybody caught on, the pair switched the game, betting people "Jake could bite a chicken's head off. He did it."

But always, Hawkins said, "I never played with a stronger man than Jake, not in college or the pros or anywhere."

You make an honest living in a world that rewards greed and unbridled ambition. You raise your children in a world that glamorizes immoral behavior and ridicules values and parental authority. You proclaim your faith in a world that idolizes itself.

Standing tall for what you believe may get you admired, but it also makes you a target for the scoffers who fear the depth of your convictions. Living the faithful life thus requires a healthy dose of physical, mental, and emotional strength.

To rely on your own strength, however, is to face the world poorly armed and woefully weak. Count on it: You will fail; the world will inevitably wear you down. Only when you admit your weakness, confess that you need some help, and allow God to be your strength will you prevail.

The strength that undergirds and supports the Christian life is not found in ourselves. Rather, it is found in the power of the Holy Spirit that lives in us.

As far as I'm concerned, being a Christian makes you more of a man.
-- Reggie White

God did not create us ten feet tall and bulletproof,
so he lends us his own power
to strengthen us in our faith walk.

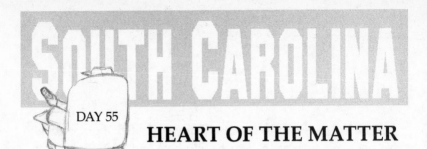

DAY 55

HEART OF THE MATTER

Read Colossians 3:1-17.

"Since, then, you have been raised with Christ, set your hearts on things above, ... Set your minds on things above, not on earthly things" (vv. 1, 2).

I wanted to do what was right in my heart." For Kip Bouknight that meant coming back to South Carolina for his senior season.

In 2000, Bouknight had what *Sports Illustrated* called "maybe the greatest season in South Carolina sports history since George Rogers ran to the Heisman Trophy." He was 17-1 with a 2.81 ERA for the SEC-champion Gamecocks, who won a school-record 56 games.

He led the nation in wins and won virtually every award a collegiate pitcher could. He was All-America, the SEC Pitcher of the Year, the SEC male athlete of the year, and the Collegiate Baseball Player of the Year. He became the first Gamecock in history to win the Golden Spikes Award, presented annually to the nation's best amateur baseball player.

When he was drafted by the Oakland A's after that sensational season, Bouknight had to decide whether to stay in school or to turn pro. He wrestled with the decision until his girlfriend told him not to worry about the money. "I kind of looked at her and said, 'What do you mean?'" Bouknight said. What she meant was that he should follow his heart and not the money. "That for me was when the decision was made," Bouknight said, because in his heart milestones, accolades, honors, and money didn't mean as much to him as pitching for the Gamecocks did.

His decision was met with much jubilation among Gamecock supporters; even the governor wrote Bouknight a letter thanking him for staying.

Following his heart, Bouknight went 10-4 his senior season. He set the school record for career strikeouts, and his 45 career wins set a school record and tied the SEC record.

As Kip Bouknight did, we often face decisions in life that force us to choose between our heart and our head. Our head says take that job with the salary increase; our heart says don't relocate because the kids are doing so well. Our head declares now is not the time to start a relationship; our heart insists that we're in love.

We wrestle with our head and our heart as we determine what matters the most to us. When it comes to the ultimate priority in our lives, though, our head *and* our heart tell us it's Jesus.

What that means for our lives is a resolution of the conflict we face daily: That of choosing between the values of our culture and a life of trust in and obedience to God. The two may occasionally be compatible, but when they're not, our head tells us what Jesus wants us to do; our heart tells us how right it is that we do it.

I wanted to do what was right in my heart and what was right was coming back.
                    -- Kip Bouknight on his decision to stay at USC

**In our struggle with competing value systems,
our head and our heart lead us to follow Jesus.**

DAY 56

WINNING

Read 1 Corinthians 15:50-58.

"[God] gives us the victory through our Lord Jesus Christ" (v. 57b).

The Gamecocks journeyed far from home in 1980 to the biggest setting in college football and came away with one of their biggest wins.

On Sept. 27, South Carolina played Michigan in Ann Arbor in front of 104,213 fans, by far the biggest crowd ever to watch a Gamecock football game. As most of the "experts" predicted, the Wolverines controlled the game in the first half, leading 14-3 at the break. Only George Rogers in his Heisman Trophy season could do much; he had 88 yards on 21 carries in the first half.

What the so-called "experts" didn't expect was that South Carolina would control the last half. The game turned early in the third quarter when Michigan was driving for what would pretty much have been a game-clinching touchdown. The Wolverine fullback fumbled into the end zone, though, and Walt Kater recovered for USC.

That big play switched momentum to the Gamecocks, and they never let go of it. They drove 80 yards with Rogers scoring from the two. Then in the fourth quarter the Wolverines gambled and lost. They faked a punt on fourth and one, and the Gamecock defense was ready. The offense took over at the Michigan 29 and took seven plays to score, Johnnie Wright getting the touchdown.

GAMECOCKS

With twelve minutes left, South Carolina led 17-14.

Defensive back Robert Perlotte then saved the game twice for USC. First, he stopped one Michigan possession with an interception. On the game's final play, Michigan went for the win from the USC three, and Perlotte deflected a pass in the end zone.

The Gamecocks were 17-14 winners and on their way to an 8-3 season and the Gator Bowl.

Life itself, not just athletic events, is a competition. You compete against all the other job or college applicants. You compete against others for a date. Sibling rivalry is real; just ask your brother or sister.

Inherent in any competition or any situation in which you strive to win is the involvement of an antagonist. You always have an opponent to overcome, even if it's an inanimate video game, a golf course, or even yourself.

Nobody wants to be numbered among life's losers. We recognize them when we see them, and maybe mutter a prayer that says something like, "There but for the grace of God go I."

But one adversary *will* defeat us: Death will claim us all. Like the Gamecocks did against Michigan, though, we can turn the tables and defeat the grave. A victory is possible, however, only through faith in Jesus Christ. With Jesus, we have hope beyond death. With Jesus, we win. For all of eternity.

I love the winning. I can take losing, but most of all, I love to play.
-- Tennis great Boris Becker

Death is the ultimate opponent;
Jesus is the ultimate victor.

DAY 57

REVELATION

Read Isaiah 53.

"But he was pierced for our transgressions, he was crushed for our iniquities; the punishment that brought us peace was upon him, and by his wounds we are healed" (v. 5).

G amecock baseball coach Ray Tanner has never claimed to be a prophet. In the 2010 College World Series, though, he had a moment that even he said was "kind of eerie."

After a loss to Oklahoma in the opening game of the series, the Gamecocks responded like the team of destiny they were with four straight wins, including the last-strike comeback against Oklahoma and the satisfying thriller that eliminated the Clemson Tigers. That last win propelled the Gamecocks into the championship finals against undefeated UCLA.

They got off to a great start by jumping out to an early three-run lead. In the third, they loaded the bases with no outs. A golden opportunity to blow the game wide open lay before them. So what happened? A short fly ball to the outfield and an out at the plate. In one pitch, USC went to no runs, two outs, and runners at second and third. That's when Tanner made his prediction.

Tanner admits he is "very much into the game when I'm in the dugout." Part of that being "into the game" was an ongoing conversation with pitching coach Mark Calvi, who in July 2010 was named the head coach at South Alabama effective in 2011.

The two coaches were standing together after the disastrous play, and Tanner said, "That didn't work out very well." "No, it didn't," Calvi replied. Then the head coach said, "The way we're going (shortstop Bobby) Haney will drive in those other two." That's exactly what he did.

With the prediction having come true, Calvi simply looked at Tanner and shook his head. USC never looked back, winning 6-1.

In our jaded age, we have pretty have relegated prophecy to dark rooms where mysterious women peer into crystal balls or clasp our sweaty palms while uttering vague generalities. At best, we understand a prophet as someone who predicts future events.

Within the pages of the Bible, though, we encounter something radically different. A prophet is a messenger from God, one who relays divine revelation to others.

Prophets seem somewhat foreign to us because in one very real sense the age of prophecy is over. In the name of Jesus, we have access to God through our prayers and through scripture. In searching for God's will for our lives, we seek divine revelation. We may speak only for ourselves and not for the greater body of Christ, but we do not need a prophet to discern what God would have us do. We need faith in the one whose birth, life, and death fulfilled more than 300 Bible prophecies.

You go through times when you just kind of feel like something is going to happen.

-- Ray Tanner on his prediction of Bobby Haney's hit

**Persons of faith continuously seek
a word from God for their lives.**

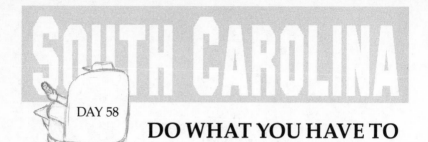

DO WHAT YOU HAVE TO

Read 2 Samuel 12:1-15a.

"The Lord sent Nathan to David" (v. 1).

Grades or jail. Alex English did what he had to, and the rest is basketball history.

English is a member of both the USC Hall of Fame and the NBA Hall of Fame. Both his collegiate and his professional jersey numbers have been retired. He played from 1973-76 in Columbia, and he remains second on the school's all-time scoring list and is third all-time in both rebounds and blocked shots. He still holds the school record for minutes played and field goals made. In the 1980s, he scored more points than any other NBA player.

All that success was a long time away when the young English stood before a judge and faced jail time. He had tried to impress a girl with his athletic skills by jumping on cars in a car lot. He didn't realize that in the process he was wreaking about $20,000 worth of havoc on the new cars he was jumping on.

He was arrested, and on his day in court the judge asked him how he was going to pay for the damage he had done. "I was a little kid. I didn't have any money," English recalled. His mother told the judge she couldn't afford to pay the damages either. The judge insisted nevertheless: Pay up or go to jail.

English began to cry as he knew what facility he would be in and how awful it was. What he didn't know was that the judge, a social worker, and his mother had worked out an agreement. He had to get As, Bs, and Cs in school; one D or F would land him in jail. "Twice a month, you'll report to your court officer," the judge said. "If you have done well, we'll let you off the hook."

"Thank you, God," English said to himself. "From that time on," he said, "I went to class and I did what I was supposed to do." He did what he had to and made the grade – for the rest of his accomplished life.

You too have had to do some things in your life that you really didn't want to do. Maybe when you put your daughter on severe restriction, broke the news of a death in the family, fired a friend, or underwent surgery. You plowed ahead because you knew it was for the best or you had no choice.

Nathan surely didn't want to confront King David and tell him what a miserable reprobate he'd been, but the prophet had no choice: Obedience to God overrode all other factors.

Of all that God asks of us in the living of a godly life, obedience is perhaps the most difficult. After all, our history of disobedience stretches all the way back to the Garden of Eden. The problem is that God expects obedience not only when his wishes match our own but also when they don't.

Obedience to God is a way of life, not a matter of convenience.

Coaching is making men do what they don't want, so they can become what they want to be.
-- Legendary NFL Coach Tom Landry

You can never foresee what God
will demand of you, but obedience requires
being ready to do whatever God asks.

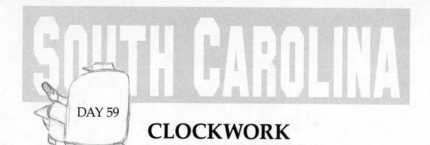

CLOCKWORK

Read Matthew 25:1-13.

"Keep watch, because you do not know the day or the hour" (v. 13).

Be late, be left."

That was the motto of USC's legendary track coach Weems Baskin, Jr.

Baskin's squads won 90 dual meets and lost only 47 during his tenure as track coach from 1949 to 1969. In 1966 as one of his first acts as athletic director, Paul Dietzel named the university's track and field facility the Weems Baskin Track. Baskin, who died in 1993, is a member of the national track and field hall of fame and the South Carolina Track Hall of Fame.

Baskin was notorious for his insistence that everyone be on time or get left behind. Tom Price related an incident in the early 1960s when the track team was to leave at 8 a.m. for a dual meet at the University of North Carolina. When three athletes were not present, Baskin gave them two minutes and then told the bus driver to pull out. About ten miles north of Columbia, a car with its horn blowing overtook the bus. "That's Billy Nies' girlfriend's car," a team member said. "Stop the bus and pick him up," Baskin ordered. Nies was the team's discus and shot-put entrant and a football tight end. Baskin's only comment was, "Good morning."

At 10 a.m., the team stopped at a restaurant about 80 miles from Columbia for a prearranged meal. As the team filed in, a

GAMECOCKS

car bearing sprinters Dean Fowble and Dick Melton showed up. Again, Baskin's only comment was a curt "Good Morning." The pair asked if they could just ride on to Chapel Hill in the car since they were almost halfway there. "That car will be here when we come back tonight," Baskin replied.

At the meet, Nies won the discus and placed third in the shot. The competition came down to the final relay race with a South Carolina team that included the two tardy sprinters. The four-man team won the event, and the Gamecocks won the meet.

We may pride ourselves on our time management, but the truth is that we don't manage time; it manages us. Hurried and harried, we live by schedules that seem to have too much what and too little when. By setting the bedside alarm at night, we even let the clock determine how much down time we get. A life of leisure actually means one in which time is of no importance.

Every second of our life – all the time we have – is a gift from God, who dreamed up time in the first place. We would do well, therefore, to consider what God considers to be good time management. After all, Jesus himself warned us against mismanaging the time we have. From God's point of view, using our time wisely means being prepared at every moment for Jesus' return, which will occur -- well, only time will tell when.

We didn't lose the game; we just ran out of time.
– Vince Lombardi

We mismanage our time when we fail to prepare for Jesus' return even though we don't know when that will be.

DAY 60

GOOD LUCK

Read 1 Samuel 28:3-20.

*"Saul then said to his attendants, 'Find me a woman who
is a medium, so I may go and inquire of her'" (v. 7).*

Chad Blackwell hopped on first base. Brendan Winn wouldn't
eat at Applebee's or Sonic for a pregame meal. The Gamecock
baseball squad of 2004 had more than its share of superstitions.

Winn may have been the most superstitious of the bunch. After
a hitless performance in the NCAA regional, he tossed out the
socks he had been wearing all season, though he did wash them
between games. "I got some new socks for this weekend," he said.
"If there's a game where I didn't do well, I change my shoes for
the next game. I might wear a different hat." Winn had some bad
games after eating his pregame meals at Applebee's and Sonic. "I
don't know if it was a coincidence the first time. But the second
time, I said, 'Never again.'"

Blackwell did a little hop on first base when he came in from
the bullpen. "It's just something that comes to you," he said. "You
do it once and you stick to it." Blackwell also wore a tiny baseball
charm that he kissed before he pitched.

Second baseman Kevin Melillo wouldn't shave his mustache
while he was on a hitting streak. With two strikes and two outs in
an inning, the Gamecock bench rubbed their caps and then took
them off and shook them for luck. Many of the players avoided
stepping on the foul line when running onto or leaving the field.

GAMECOCKS

Not everybody on the team was superstitious, though. Outfielder Davy Gregg just laughed at his teammates' quirks. "I think it's a little crazy sometimes," he said.

And how did this particularly superstitious bunch of Gamecocks do? With a lot of talent and maybe a little luck along the way, they went 53-17 and won the super regional and three games in the College World Series.

Black cats are right pretty. A medium is a steak. A key chain with a rabbit's foot wasn't too lucky for the rabbit. And what in the world is a blarney stone? About as superstitious as you get is to say "God bless you" when somebody sneezes.

You look indulgently upon good-luck charms, tarot cards, astrology, palm readers, and the like; they're really just amusing and harmless. So what's the problem? Nothing as long as you conduct yourself with the belief that superstitious objects and rituals – from broken mirrors to your daily horoscope – can't bring about good or bad luck. You aren't willing to let such notions and nonsense rule your life.

The danger of superstition lies in its ability to lure you into trusting it, thus allowing it some degree of influence over your life. In that case, it subverts God's rightful place.

Whether or not it's superstition, something does rule your life. It should be God – and God alone.

I'd use the same bat all year if I could.

-- *Superstitious Brendan Winn*

Superstitions may not rule your life, but something does; it should be God and God alone.

TRICK PLAYS

Read Acts 19:11-20.

"The evil spirit answered them, 'Jesus I know, and I know about Paul, but who are you?'" (v. 15)

One of the most exciting games in the South Carolina-Clemson series is remembered not for its bizarre, game-winning touchdown but for one of the best pranks ever pulled on an opponent.

On Nov. 11, 1961, in Columbia, Clemson led 14-13 in the fourth quarter when USC's Dickie Day smashed into the line but had the ball squirt out of his hands. It sailed right into the clutches of quarterback Jimmy Costen, who took off down the sideline for a touchdown. The Gamecocks held on for a 21-14 win.

Before the game, though, the crowd was settling in when the orange-clad Tigers, led by their longtime coach Frank Howard, trotted onto the field. The Clemson fans yelled, their cannon boomed, the band broke into "Tiger Rag," and the players circled up for calisthenics.

Instead of doing the side-straddle hop, though, they did the bunny hop and "stumbled, bumbled, and fell all over each other." They paired off with one player using his fingers to simulate an udder and the other milking them. A center snapped a ball 40 yards over the head of a punter, who retrieved the ball and kicked it backwards. Players blew kisses to the stands. Coach Howard walked around and spit tobacco juice all over the place.

The Tiger fans had been had. As John Chandler Griffin put it,

GAMECOCKS

"Those trusting Clemson bumpkins had once again fallen victim to a cruel city-slicker hoax." A group of USC fraternity boys had borrowed uniforms from a high school and "managed to pull off one of the most delightful pranks in the history of the series." For some reason, however, the targets of the farce did not seem particularly amused.

Scam artists are everywhere, pulling tricks that aren't as funny or as harmless as the great pregame prank of 1961. An e-mail encourages you to send money to some foreign country to get rich. That guy at your front door offers to resurface your driveway at a ridiculously low price. A TV ad promises a pill to help you lose weight without diet or exercise.

You've been around; you check things out before deciding. The same approach is necessary with spiritual matters too because false religions and bogus Christian denominations abound. The key is what any group does with Jesus. Is he the son of God, the ruler of the universe, and the only way to salvation? If not, then what the group espouses is something other than the true Word of God.

The good news about Jesus does indeed sound too good to be true. But the only catch is that there is no catch. No trick -- just the truth.

When you run trick plays and they work, you're a genius. But when they don't work, folks question your sanity.
-- Bobby Bowden

God's promises through Jesus sound too good to be true, but the only catch is that there is no catch.

SOUTH CAROLINA

DAY 62

FOOD FOR THOUGHT

Read Genesis 9:1-7.

"Everything that lives and moves will be food for you. Just as I gave you the green plants, I now give you everything" *(v. 3).*

A soft ice cream machine – that's what it took to keep another school from stealing one of the most valuable members of the South Carolina athletic department.

She was Sue Kurpiewski, the dietician in charge of feeding Gamecock athletes. She was hired by Paul Dietzel in 1967 when the Roost was built. She did such a good job that several years after he returned to LSU, Dietzel tried to hire her. Coach Jim Carlen asked what it would take to keep her, and she said if Carlen "would buy her a soft ice cream machine so she could make ice cream for the boys, she would stay." The next day business manager John Moore had a memo, and soft ice cream became a daily feature at the Roost. Kurpiewski stayed until she retired in 1988; she was feted on the field at a home football game.

She often prepared special dishes for her boys. For instance, Jeff Grantz liked macaroni and cheese but only with Velveeta. He got Velveeta. Heisman-Trophy winner George Rogers preferred fried bologna rather than steak for his pregame meals, and he always did prefer meatloaf to steak. Basketball player Kenny Reynolds preferred hamburger to steak.

Freddie Chalmers (football 1981-82) once asked Mrs. K why

she didn't have neck bones on the menu. "I went out and bought some neck bones," she said. "After that, we had them about twice a year."

Moore once said about Mrs. K and the food she fixed for her boys, she was the "only person I know who could overspend an unlimited budget." Funny thing about that: the players sure never seemed to mind.

Belly up to the buffet, boys and girls, for barbecue, sirloin steak, grilled chicken, and fried catfish with hush puppies. Rachael Ray's a household name; hamburger joints, pizza parlors, and taco stands lurk on every corner; and we have a TV channel devoted exclusively to food. We love our chow.

Food is one of God's really good ideas, but consider the complex divine plan that begins with a seed and ends with French fries. The creator of all life devised a system in which living things are sustained and nourished physically through the sacrifice of other living things in a way similar to what Christ underwent to save you spiritually. Whether it's fast food or home-cooked, everything you eat is a gift from God secured through a divine plan in which some plants and animals have given up their lives.

Pausing to give thanks before we dive in seems the least we can do.

I cut down to six meals a day.

-- Charles Barkley on losing weight

God created a system that nourishes us through the sacrifice of other living things; that's worth a thank-you.

DAY 63

YOU NEVER KNOW

Read Exodus 3:1-12.

"But Moses said to God, 'Who am I, that I should go to Pharaoh and bring the Israelites out of Egypt?' And God said, 'I will be with you'" (vv. 11-12a).

The greatest player in South Carolina fast-pitch softball history never even played the game until she arrived in Columbia.

Tiff Tootle was "a competitive blonde softball player from Reidsville, Ga.," who was a sensational talent. The problem was that her high school had played only slow-pitch softball, and in the late 1980s and early 1990s, the colleges were switching to the fast-pitch game. She was willing to give it a try, though, because she wanted to play.

"My dad made a video; we sent it to coach (hall of famer Joyce Compton); I came on an official visit, and it all worked out from there," Tootle recalled.

Tootle didn't know how she would fare in this different game, but to say it "worked out" is an understatement. Compton took Tootle's natural skills and innate competitive nature and molded one of the finest softball players in collegiate history.

The bare statistics reveal just how well it all worked out. In her career from 1990-93, Tootle was a three-time All-America. She set NCAA records for hits and runs scored for a career and for a single season in 1992. She remains South Carolina's all-time leader in runs, hits, batting average, on-base percentage, and stolen bases.

She hit more than .400 all four seasons, finishing her career with a .432 batting average, at the time the best in NCAA history.

Tootle's success carried over to her team as in 1991 and 1992, the Gamecocks posted back-to-back 50-win seasons. "It was awesome to be able to play and have that team success," Tootle said.

And all that success came from someone who had never played the game before.

You never know what you can do until – like Tiff Tootle -- you want to bad enough or until -- like Moses -- you have to. Serving in the military, maybe even in combat. Standing by a friend while everyone else unjustly excoriates her. Undergoing agonizing medical treatment and managing to smile. You never know what life will demand of you.

It's that way too in your relationship with God. As Moses discovered, you never know where or when God will call you or what God will ask of you. You do know that God expects you to be faithful and willing to trust him even when he calls you to tasks that daunt and dismay you.

You can respond confidently to whatever God calls you to do for him. That's because even though you never know what lies ahead, you do know that God will both lead you and provide what you need.

There's one word to describe baseball: You never know.

– Yogi Berra

**You never know what God will ask you to do,
but you always know he will provide everything
you need to do it.**

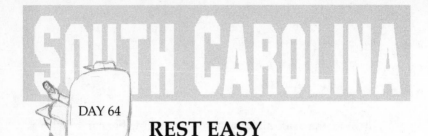

DAY 64

REST EASY

Read Hebrews 4:1-11.

*"There remains, then, a Sabbath rest for the people of God;
for anyone who enters God's rest also rests from his own
work, just as God did from his. Let us, therefore, make
every effort to enter that rest" (vv. 9-11).*

Athletes need rest before a game, but often they're too keyed
up to rest easy. Gamecock safety Bryant Gilliard never had that
problem; he had a surefire way of relaxing.

Gilliard was a senior cocaptain in 1984, the year of the "Fire
Ants and Black Magic," South Carolina's best team ever. In one of
the biggest games of the year, Gilliard had a game every defensive
back dreams of and few ever achieve.

The Gamecocks were 8-0 and ranked No. 5 when they hosted
No. 11 FSU in what turned out to be a 38-26 shootout, the win
keyed – despite all those points – by the defense, which forced
seven Seminole turnovers. Gilliard got four of those turnovers
himself: He intercepted four passes.

"My goal had been to get one interception per game," he
recalled. He got that early, then a second, and then a third, this
one in the end zone. His fourth pick "was probably my favorite
one," he said. "I really had to go up and out-jump the receiver."
For his incredible performance, *Sports Illustrated* named Gilliard
the national defensive player of the week.

He was certainly ready to play, which included being well-rested, but Gilliard was always rested for a game. In fact, someone usually had to wake him up to play. What was his secret? He read the Bible. "That is where I seek comfort," he said. "But what it also does for me . . . is relax me. It relaxes me to the point that prior to a game, someone usually has to wake me up. I sleep the entire time."

As part of the natural rhythm of life, rest is important to maintain physical health, even for non-athletes. Rest has different images, though: a good eight hours in the sack; a Saturday morning that begins in the backyard with the paper and a pot of coffee; a vacation in the mountains where the most strenuous thing you do is change position in the hot tub.

Rest is also part of the rhythm and the health of our spiritual lives. Often we envision the faithful person as always busy, always doing something for God whether it's teaching Sunday school or showing up at church every time the doors open.

But God himself rested from work, and in blessing us with the Sabbath, he calls us into a time of rest. To rest by simply spending time in the presence of God is to receive spiritual revitalization and rejuvenation. Sleep refreshes your body and your mind; God's rest refreshes your soul.

You have peace of mind and can enjoy yourself, get more sleep, and rest when you know that it was a one hundred percent effort that you gave – win or lose.

-- *NHL legend Gordie Howe*

**God promises you a spiritual rest
that renews and refreshes your soul.**

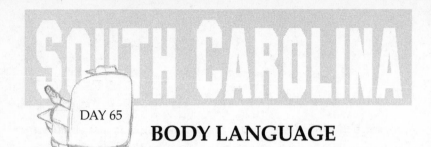

DAY 65

BODY LANGUAGE

Read 1 Corinthians 6:12-20.

"Do you not know that your body is a temple of the Holy Spirit, who is in you, whom you have received from God? . . . Honor God with your body" (vv. 19, 20b).

When she was in elementary school in her native Hungary, Petra Ujhelyi's body was so different from the rest of the students that they taunted and ridiculed her. So she beat them up.

What made Ujhelyi different was her height; she was significantly and noticeably taller than everybody else. The giraffe jokes and the name-calling were "so bad I didn't want to go to school," she recalled. "I didn't want to go to the playground."

But Ujhelyi eventually discovered that her height was quite an advantage on the basketball court, especially when she began to practice with the men's club team her father coached. By then, all the name-calling had stopped since "it's tough to talk trash to a girl when she's pulling down rebounds and scoring over you."

Not only did basketball change the guys' reaction to Ujhelyi's height, it also changed her perspective about her body. On the court, she said, "It wasn't a big deal that [I was] tall. Now I'm cool with it."

Nothing changed when Ujhelyi arrived in Columbia in 1999. At 6-4, she was still taller than most guys, only now they were college students who didn't tease her. Instead, they went to watch her play, especially to watch her rebound. Starting at center and nicknamed "the Big Peezy" by her teammates, Ujhelyi sealed off the lane for two of USC's best teams ever, the 25-7 squad of 2001-02 and the 23-8 team of her senior season. As a senior, she became more of a scoring threat, averaging 11.7 points per game.

Interestingly, she was never an elbow-throwing ruffian on the court, perhaps because nobody was taunting her about her size anymore. They were just intimidated by it.

Your body may never have been the object of ridicule as Petra Ujhelyi's was in her childhood, but most of us still don't see a body beautiful when we look into a mirror. Too heavy, too short, too pale — there's always something wrong because we compare ourselves to an impossible standard Hollywood and fashion magazines have created, and we are inevitably disappointed.

God must have been quite partial to your body, though, because he personally fashioned it and gave it to you free of charge. Your body, like everything else in your life, is thus a gift from God. But God didn't stop there. He then quite voluntarily chose to inhabit your body, sharing it with you in the person of the Holy Spirit.

What an act of consummate ungratefulness it is then to abuse your God-given body by violating God's standards for living. To do so is in fact to dishonor God.

If you don't do what's best for your body, you're the one who comes up on the short end.

-- *Julius Erving*

**You may not have a fine opinion of your body,
but God thought enough of it
to personally create it for you.**

DAY 66

HERO WORSHIP

Read 1 Samuel 16:1-13.

"Do not consider his appearance or his height, for . . . the Lord does not look at the things man looks at. . . . The Lord looks at the heart" (v. 7).

South Carolina – both the school and the state – was desperate for a local hero," wrote *Sports Illustrated*. For a brief period, they found him in Joe Morrison.

Morrison was the Gamecocks' head football coach from 1983-88. He guided the 1984 "Black Magic and Fire Ants" team to a 10-2 record, the most wins in school history, and a No. 11 ranking, the highest in school history. The teams of 1987 and '88 had back-to-back eight-win bowl seasons.

His teams whipped Southern Cal, Notre Dame, Georgia, Pittsburgh, Florida State, and Clemson. In 1984, he was the Walter Camp Foundation's National Coach of the Year. Linebacker James Seawright and offensive lineman Del Wilkes were first-team All-Americas in 1984, and Sterling Sharpe, Brad Edwards, Harold Green, Robert Brooks, and Todd Ellis all played for him.

His legacy is still in place in Columbia. Part of it is the wearing of black uniforms. Morrison showed up for a press conference in all black because his other coaching gear had not arrived; "it was clean and it fit," he explained. Starting in 1987, black became the primary jersey for home games. In 1983, he instituted the playing of *Einleitung* from *Also Sprach Zarathustra* for the team entrance.

GAMECOCKS

Morrison's heroic status is undoubtedly enhanced by his untimely death of a heart attack at 51 on Feb. 5, 1989, and that he didn't achieve fame somewhere else first. "Joe Morrison did it at the highest level – at South Carolina," Ellis said. "Those who recognize that still look at him as the benchmark."

Decades after his death, Joe Morrison is still the standard against which others are measured.

A hero is not only someone who performs brave and dangerous feats that save or protect someone's life, but also a person who is admired for exploits and accomplishments. While the latter fits Joe Morrison, you may well figure that either definition excludes you.

But ask your son about that when you show him how to bait a hook, or your daughter when you show up for her dance recital. Look into the eyes of those Little Leaguers you help coach.

Ask God about heroism when you're steady in your faith. For God, a hero is a person with the heart of a servant. And if a hero is a servant who acts to save other's lives, then the greatest hero of all is Jesus Christ.

God seeks heroes today, those who will proclaim the name of their hero – Jesus – proudly and boldly, no matter how others may scoff or ridicule. God knows heroes when he sees them -- by what's in their hearts.

Heroes and cowards feel exactly the same fear; heroes just act differently.
-- Boxing trainer Cus D'Amato

**God's heroes are those who remain steady
in their faith while serving others.**

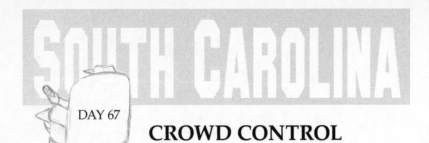
DAY 67

CROWD CONTROL

Read Hebrews 11:39-12:2.

"Therefore, since we are surrounded by such a great cloud of witnesses, . . . let us run with perseverance the race marked out for us" (v. 12:1).

Some tickets were bogus. Some tickets were real. And nobody could tell the difference.

In 1946, two brothers printed and sold thousands of bogus tickets for Big Thursday's Clemson game. They were arrested the Tuesday before the game, but they had done such a good job that nobody could tell which tickets were real and which were not. The result was a legendary fiasco.

Shortly before game time, about 35,000 ticket holders swarmed around Memorial Stadium, which had been recently expanded to hold 26,000. Soon the stadium was full and the gates were closed. That left thousands of fans, many of whom held legitimate tickets, more than irritated about the whole business and determined to see the game. They simply rushed the gates, "battering them to the ground, then swarmed into the stadium like killer bees."

Furman Bisher wrote, "You couldn't see anything but the playing field, and not all of that" because the crowd on the sidelines was dozens deep. Clemson's Coach Frank Howard said, "I'd look around for a substitute and there'd be fifty people between me and my bench. It was almost impossible to do any coaching."

Even dignitaries couldn't see. Jimmy Byrnes, who was then the

GAMECOCKS

Secretary of State under Harry Truman, said he gave up his box seat when fans piled in and made his way down to the field where he "got down on his hands and knees, then watched the game from between the legs of Carolina players on the sideline."

The Gamecocks scored twice in the fourth quarter to win the best game that most in the crowd never saw 26-14.

You don't have a huge crowd of folks applauding your efforts every day, and you certainly don't have people battering down gates in a rush to witness your every move. Sometimes you may even feel alone. A child's illness, the slow death of a loved one, financial troubles, worries about your health – you feel isolated.

But a person of faith is never alone, and not just because you're aware of God's presence. You are always surrounded by a crowd of God's most faithful witnesses, those in the present and those from the past. Their faithfulness both encourages and inspires. They, too, have faced the difficult circumstances with which you contend, and they remained faithful and true to God.

With their examples before you, you can endure your trials, looking in hope and faithfulness beyond your immediate troubles to God's glorious future. Your final victory in Christ will be even sweeter because of your struggles.

A very small crowd here today. I can count the people on one hand. Can't be more than 30.

– Announcer Michael Abrahamson

The person of faith is surrounded by a crowd of witnesses whose faithfulness in difficult times inspires us to remain true to God no matter what.

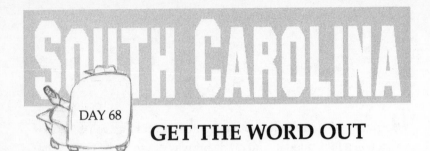

DAY 68

GET THE WORD OUT

Read Mark 1:21-28.

"News about him spread quickly over the whole region"
(v. 28).

Sometimes it takes only one response to make an advertising effort a success. That's the way it was for Dan Phillips.

During his junior year in high school in Michigan, Phillips conducted a campaign to secure himself a swimming scholarship. He sent letters to about fifty schools. The results were not overwhelming. "I never even heard from a lot of them," he said. "The majority of the ones that did respond sent your average form letter – 'Thanks for your interest in our program,' that sort of thing."

He did get a personal response from USC coach Keith Switzer, but even the head Gamecock wasn't particularly impressed at the time. Phillips "was just an average high school swimmer," Switzer said. But the two met and made a connection, and Phillips got his scholarship.

The result was one of the greatest swimmers in USC history. "We were lucky," Switzer said. It turned out Phillips was "pretty talented and a hard worker. When you combine those two attributes in this sport, you can go a long way."

Phillips did. He was a three-time All-America and was the team captain in 1994 and 1995. In 1995, he was the SEC champion in the 200-yard freestyle. He won a gold medal in the 800-meter freestyle relay in the 1993 World University Games. After he graduated, he went into coaching, returning to Columbia for two seasons as an assistant coach before moving on to Ohio State. He also won a gold medal and a silver medal in the 1999 Pan American Games.

During and after his career at South Carolina, Dan Phillips had no need to advertise. His performance did all the promoting for him.

Commercials, promotions, and advertisements for products and services inundate us. Turn on your computer: ads pop up. Watch NASCAR: decals cover the cars and the drivers' uniforms. TV, radio, newspapers, magazines, billboards -- everyone's trying to get the word out the best way possible.

Jesus was no different in that he used the most effective and efficient means of advertising he had at his disposal to spread his message of salvation and hope among the masses. That was word of mouth. In his ministry, Jesus didn't isolate himself; instead, he moved from town to town among everyday folks, preaching, teaching, and healing. Those who encountered Jesus then told others about their experience.

Almost two millennia later, nothing's really changed. Speaking to someone else about Jesus remains the best way to get the word out, and the best advertisement of all is a changed life.

[Coach Switzer] was the only one who left a message at the hotel saying he'd like to see me.
-- Dan Phillips on the results of his advertising campaign

The best advertising for Jesus is word of mouth, telling others what he has done for you.

FAMILY TIES

Read Mark 3:31-35.

*"[Jesus] said, 'Here are my mother and my brothers!
Whoever does God's will is my brother and sister and
mother'" (vv. 34-35).*

George Rogers' family had apparently doomed him. Ultimately, though, it rescued him.

Rogers is the most famous football player in South Carolina history; he even has a road by Williams-Brice Stadium named for him. He won the 1980 Heisman Trophy, and he was the first USC player in history to have his jersey retired while he was still playing.

Such excellence seemed unlikely, though, when Rogers was a child. His father left when George was six; he was later convicted of murder. His family moved from one housing project in Georgia to another, "always one step ahead of the landlord." Rogers' clothes were little more than rags; he wanted to play football but he didn't have the $2 for insurance.

When he was a teenager, Rogers often skipped class and lied about his age "so he could weed fields and sweep warehouses for $1.80 an hour." "I used to cry myself to sleep," he said, "but I never felt like giving up."

Then his family saved his life. Just before his sophomore year, he moved in with Otella Rogers in Duluth, Ga. Her brother-in-law was George's grandfather. "I told him if he wanted to be something, I'd help," she said. So she taught young George to fix his own breakfast and to do his own laundry. She gave him a stable home for the first time in his life, and – equally important – she made sure that he went to school every day. In Duluth's third game of Rogers' sophomore season, the starting halfback broke a wrist. Rogers replaced him and scored four touchdowns. With support from his family, he was on his way.

Some wit said families are like fudge, mostly sweet with a few nuts. You can probably call the names of your sweetest relatives, whom you cherish, and of the nutty ones too, whom you mostly try to avoid at a family reunion.

Like it or not, you have a family, and that's God's doing. God cherishes the family so much that he chose to live in one as a son, a brother, and a cousin.

One of Jesus' more startling actions was to redefine the family. No longer is it a single household of blood relatives or even a clan or a tribe. Jesus' family is the result not of an accident of birth but rather a conscious choice. All those who do God's will are members of Jesus' family.

What a startling and wonderful thought! You have family members out there you don't even know who stand ready to love you just because you're part of God's family.

There are three things in my life which I really love: God, my family, and baseball.

-- *Author Al Gallagher*

For followers of Jesus, family comes not from a shared ancestry but from a shared faith.

DAY 70

DRY RUN

Read John 4:1-25.

"Everyone who drinks this water will be thirsty again,
but whoever drinks the water I give him will never thirst.
Indeed, the water I give him will become in him a spring
of water welling up to eternal life" (vv. 13-14).

Gamecock fans "danced in the aisles, they cheered wildly, and at the final gun, they threw a wild, raucous celebration of unadulterated relief two years (and two coaches) in the making." The drought was over.

On Sept. 2, 2000, at Williams-Brice Stadium, the Gamecocks trounced New Mexico State 31-0, ending 21 weekends in which "South Carolina had known only sorrow, frustration, disappointment." That's because the Gamecocks had experienced a drought of biblical proportions; it lasted for two years and 21 games. And on this night, it ended. Fans so anticipated the drought breaker that with 36 seconds left, a bunch of them "stormed the north goal posts with celebration, and destruction, in mind."

"I'm proud of the team," Coach Lou Holtz said. "We looked like a football team today."

Quarterback Phil Petty led the win. "I thought he played brilliantly," Holtz said. Tailback Derek Watson ran for 114 yards on 14 carries, his first touchdown as a Gamecock coming on a leap into the end zone with 10:04 left in the first half. The touchdown made it 14-0 and put the drought on life support.

GAMECOCKS

Safety Willie Offord then struck the final blow with an interception that set up Reid Bethea's 24-yard field goal. The defense even scored a touchdown; linebacker Andre Offing gobbled up a fumble and chugged 23 yards for the score.

"This is a starting point," said receiver Jermale Kelly. He was right as the Gamecocks were on their way back from the long time in the wilderness. The drought and the goal posts went down on this night of celebration, victory, and relief.

You can walk across that river you boated on in the spring. The city's put all neighborhoods on water restriction, and that beautiful lawn you fertilized and seeded will turn a sickly, pale green and may lapse all the way to brown. Somebody wrote "Wash Me" on the rear window of your truck.

The sun bakes everything, including the concrete. The earth itself seems exhausted, just barely hanging on. It's a drought.

It's the way a soul looks that shuts God out.

God instilled thirst in us to warn us of our body's need for physical water. He also gave us a spiritual thirst that can be quenched only by his presence in our lives. Without God, we are like tumbleweeds, dried out and windblown, offering the illusion of life where there is only death.

Living water – water of life – is readily available in Jesus. We may drink our fill, and thus we slake our thirst and end our soul's drought – forever.

Drink before you are thirsty. Rest before you are tired.
-- Paul de Vivie, father of French cycle touring

Our souls thirst for God's refreshing presence.

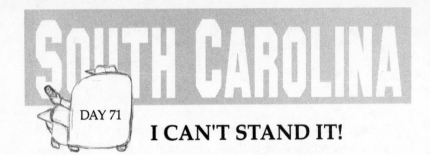
DAY 71

I CAN'T STAND IT!

Read Exodus 32:1-20.

"[Moses'] anger burned and he threw the tablets out of his hands, breaking them to pieces at the foot of the mountain" (v. 19).

A coach flopped onto his back to protest a call. Two players pushed and shoved each other. A Gamecock player got into an argument with an opposing team's coach. How's that for frustration? And all in the last 2:11 of one of USC's wildest finishes ever.

Dave Odom's Gamecocks of 2003-04 went 23-11 and earned a berth in the NCAA tournament. On Jan. 24, 2004, they were in trouble against LSU, which led 50-47 with 2:11 left to play and had the ball. USC had had a frustrating night, missing its first 22 3-point shots. But in those last 2:11, the game got wild, woolly, wacky -- and frustrating.

Gamecock Mike Boynton drew a charging call on a play that occurred right in front of the LSU bench. The Tiger head coach, who had been watching the play from his knees, fell to his back and stretched out his legs in frustration. That drew a technical foul call from an official who didn't think much of the coach's histrionics.

"That was the turning point," USC's Carlos Powell said. "Him getting hyped up like that only helped us." Josh Gonner sank one of the two free throws to ignite an 11-2 Gamecock run and a 58-52 lead with only 21.1 seconds left.

GAMECOCKS

That's when Rolando Howell and a Tiger got entangled at the free throw line, which escalated into a pushing and shoving match that drew a double technical foul from the refs. The frustration continued to boil over when Boynton and an LSU assistant coach started jawing and Boynton drew a technical foul.

When the final whistle had sounded and the wackiness was over, the Gamecocks had a wild – if at times frustrating – 61-55 SEC win.

The traffic light catches you when you're running late for work or your doctor's appointment. The bureaucrat gives you red tape when you want assistance. Your daughter refuses to take her homework seriously. Makes your blood boil, doesn't it?

Frustration is part of God's testing ground that is life even if much of what frustrates us today results from man-made organizations, bureaucracies, and machines. What's important is not that you encounter frustration—that's a given—but how you handle it. Do you respond with curses, screams, and violence? Or with a deep breath, a silent prayer, and calm persistence, and patience?

It may be difficult to imagine Jesus stuck in traffic or waiting for hours in a long line in a government office. It is not difficult, however, to imagine how he would act in such situations, and, thus, to know exactly how you should respond. No matter how frustrated you are.

I got caught up in the heat of the battle.
-- Mike Boynton on the frustration that led him to jaw with a coach

Frustration is a vexing part of life,
but God expects us to handle it gracefully.

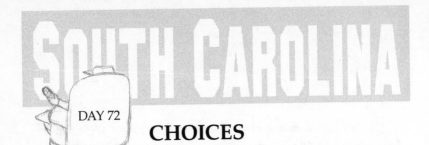

DAY 72

CHOICES

Read Deuteronomy 30:15-20.

*"I have set before you life and death, blessings and curses.
Now choose life, so that you and your children may live"*
(v. 19).

Mark Love had a choice to make: stay or go. Either choice would forever change his life.

Love made it through the extremely difficult process of getting into the Naval Academy. He endured two years of the most grueling training in the world and had his sights set on the Navy SEALs program. His career as a naval officer was assured. He was also successful on the football field; he played in 22 games in 1993 and '94, starting four as a sophomore with 69 tackles. He would be a starting linebacker in 1995. To use a naval phrase, everything was smooth sailing for Love.

But then he learned that his mother had been diagnosed with diabetes, which had led to the death of both of her parents and an uncle. Love's parents were nine hours driving time away in South Carolina. So he had a choice: stay at the Naval Academy or transfer to South Carolina so he could be closer to his mother. The first choice meant giving up valuable time with her; the latter meant giving up his military career and his football scholarship.

For Love, it was really no choice. "I just made it up in my mind that I wanted to be around her more," he said. "My parents are really involved in my life. My mom is my best friend."

GAMECOCKS

So he chose his mother and South Carolina, walking on in 1995 and sitting out a season as a transfer. He was so good on the scout team defense, though, that Coach Brad Scott awarded him a scholarship before the 1996 season. He played little, however, primarily on special teams, making two tackles.

Five games into the 1997 season, Love got his chance when senior starter Shane Burnham, the team's leading tackler, broke a hand. Love got the start at middle linebacker, perhaps as a reward both for his talent and for the heartfelt choice he had made.

As with Mark Love, your life is the sum of the choices you've made. That is, you have arrived at this moment and this place in your life because of the choices you made in your past. Your love of the Gamecocks. Your spouse or the absence of one. Mechanic, teacher, or beautician. A condo in Charleston or a ranch home in Aiken. Dog, cat, or goldfish. You chose; you live with the results.

That includes the most important choice you will ever have to make: faith or the lack of it. That we have the ability to make decisions when faced with alternatives is a gift from God, who allows that faculty even when he's part of the choice. We can choose whether or not we will love him. God does remind us that this particular choice has rather extreme consequences: Choosing God's way is life; choosing against him is death.

Life or death. What choice is that?

The choices you make in life make you.

-- *John Wooden*

God gives you the freedom to choose: life or death; what kind of choice is that?

DAY 73

TEARS IN HEAVEN

Read Revelation 21:1-8.

*"[God] will wipe every tear from their eyes. There will be
no more death or mourning or crying or pain" (v. 4).*

When Earl Bass left the mound for the last time as a Gamecock,
he wouldn't tip his cap to the crowd that gave him a standing
ovation. He wasn't been rude; he just didn't want everyone to see
his tears.

Bass is among South Carolina's greatest pitchers ever. He was
5-1 as a freshman in 1972, 12-1 in 1974, and 17-1 in 1975 and was
All-America in both 1974 and '75. He pitched only eight innings in
1973 because of tendinitis.

In the championship game of the NCAA regional in 1975, Bass
made his only relief appearance of the season. He retired ten
straight batters before issuing a walk with two outs in the ninth.
When his first baseman called time and walked over to the mound,
Bass told him to get back to first base "and put your glove in your
pocket, because this guy is mine." Bass struck the batter out, and
the Gamecocks were on their way to Omaha and the College
World Series for the first time.

The Gamecocks advanced all the way to the championship
game against Texas when, pitching on only two days' rest, Bass
lost 5-1. When Coach Bobby Richardson came out to the mound
and asked for the ball, Bass couldn't believe it. "He can't mean
me," Bass remembered thinking. "You did your best, and that's

all anyone can ask," Richardson said. That's when the tears came as Bass realized he would not bring a championship home to Columbia.

He and Richardson walked off the mound together, and the Omaha crowd rose in tribute. "Tip your cap," Richardson said, but Bass didn't. His tears wouldn't let him.

When your parents died. When a friend told you she was divorcing. When you broke your collarbone. When you watch a sad movie.

You cry. Crying is as much a part of life as are breathing and indigestion. Usually our tears are brought on by pain, disappointment, or sorrow.

But what about the night your first child was born? When South Carolina beats Clemson? When you surrendered your life to Jesus? Those times elicit tears too; we cry at the times of our greatest, most overwhelming joy.

Thus, while there will be tears in Heaven, they will only be tears of sheer, unmitigated, undiluted joy. The greatest joy possible, a joy beyond our imagining, must occur when we finally see Christ. If we shed tears when the Gamecocks win a football game, can we really believe that we will stand dry-eyed and calm in the presence of Jesus?

What we will not shed in Heaven are tears of sorrow and pain.

I didn't want them to know I had been crying.
-- Earl Bass on not tipping his cap to the crowd

Tears in Heaven will be like everything else there: a part of the joy we will experience.

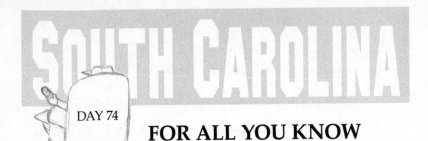

DAY 74

FOR ALL YOU KNOW

Read John 8:12-32.

"You will know the truth, and the truth will set you free"
(v. 32).

If I'd have known how important it would have been later in life to win that last game, I'd have been so scared I wouldn't have been able to take the snap," Tommy Suggs said. But he didn't know, so he wasn't scared, and he did win that last game.

Suggs is perhaps best known to today's Gamecock fans as the color commentator for the Gamecock Radio Network. His former coach, Paul Dietzel, heard Suggs speak at several Fellowship of Christian Athletes meetings, liked his style, and recommended him for the job. From 1968-70, though, Suggs quarterbacked the Gamecocks well enough to be inducted into the athletic hall of fame in 1989. He also did something no other quarterback in South Carolina football history has done before or since. And that's where that last game comes in.

Against Clemson in 1970, Suggs certainly started out as if he were scared; he threw three interceptions in the first half. "Tom, you're eight for eight, three to them and five to us," Dietzel told him at halftime. Suggs recovered to throw three touchdown passes the last half, and the Gamecocks whipped the Tigers 38-32.

His last touchdown was an audible to his friend, receiver Jimmy Mitchell. As Suggs remembered it, the Gamecocks were at the 34 when both Mitchell and he saw the defensive coverage: a sure touchdown if Suggs threw to Mitchell. The signal was to touch the face mask, and Mitchell was so excited, Suggs said, he was "about to shake his helmet off making sure I saw it."

What was it Suggs did that he didn't know about or he might have been too nervous to accomplish it? With that 1970 win, he went 4-0 against Clemson including his freshman team's win.

Unlike Tommy Suggs, you may know you're making history as you do it, but there's still much you just flat don't know. Maybe it's the formula for the area of a cylinder or the capital of Myanmar. You may not know how they make paper out of trees. Or how toothpaste gets into the tube. And can you honestly say you know how the opposite sex thinks?

Despite your ignorance about certain subjects, you manage quite well because what you don't know generally doesn't hurt you too much. In certain aspects of your life, though, ignorance is anything but harmless. Imagine, for instance, the consequence of not knowing how to do your job. Or of getting behind the wheel without knowing how to drive a car.

And in your faith life, what you don't know can have awful, eternal consequences. To willfully choose not to know Jesus is to be condemned to an eternity apart from God. When it comes to Jesus, knowing the truth sets you free; ignoring the truth enslaves you.

It's what you learn after you know it all that counts.

— John Wooden

What you don't know may not hurt you
except when it comes to Jesus.

DAY 75

UNEXPECTEDLY

Read Luke 2:1-20.

"She gave birth to her firstborn, a son. She wrapped him in cloths and placed him in a manger, because there was no room for them in the inn" (v. 7).

The bookies and the bettors had it all figured out: Virginia would whip South Carolina by at least fourteen points. And the game went exactly as expected – except for 1:45 of the fourth quarter.

The Oyster Bowl of 1952 was a Shrine-sponsored charity game played on Nov. 1 in Norfolk, Va. The Cavaliers were 4-1 and had pitched three shutouts while the Gamecocks were 3-2 with big losses to Army and to Duke.

Virginia controlled the game just as the experts had expected, taking a 14-0 lead midway through the fourth quarter. But then Gamecock Coach Rex Enright did something unexpected: He benched his starting quarterback in favor of backup Dick Balka, a senior who had transferred from Notre Dame and had played very little.

Balka missed his first two passes, but then he hit three in a row, the last a 25-yard touchdown toss to Walt Shea. With 6:30 to play, South Carolina trailed only 14-7.

Virginia fumbled the kickoff, and Bob Korn recovered for the Gamecocks at the six. Three plays later, Mike Caskey scored from the one. Suddenly and unexpectedly, the game was tied.

A penalty on the ensuing kickoff backed the Cavs up to their own six. Gene Witt caused a fumble, and Bob King fell on the football in the end zone for a touchdown. South Carolina had scored three touchdowns in only 1:45 to win 21-14. Jake Penland called it "an almost unbelievable finish to a game that started out mildly and continued that way into the fourth quarter."

It was certainly an unexpected finish.

Just like the experts and the 1952 USC-Virginia game, we think we've got everything figured out and planned for, and then something unexpected happens. Someone gets ill; you fall in love; you lose your job; you're going to have another child. Life surprises us with its bizarre twists and turns.

God is that way too, catching us unawares to remind us he's still around. A friend who hears you're down and stops by, a child's laugh, an achingly beautiful sunset -- unexpected moments of love and beauty. God is like that, always doing something in our lives we didn't expect.

But why shouldn't he? There is nothing God can't do. The only factor limiting what God can do is the paucity of our own faith.

Expect the unexpected from God, this same deity who unexpectedly came to live among us as a man. He does, by the way, expect a response from you.

Sports is about adapting to the unexpected and being able to modify plans at the last minute.
– Sir Roger Bannister, first-ever sub-four-minute miler

God does the unexpected to remind you
of his presence -- like showing up as Jesus –
and now he expects a response from you.

DAY 76

BAD IDEA

Read Mark 14:43-50.

*"The betrayer had arranged a signal with them: 'The one
I kiss is the man; arrest him and lead him away under
guard'" (v. 44).*

The University of South Carolina Board of Trustees once had
an idea so bad that if they pulled it off today they would stand a
good chance of being tarred and feathered while they were being
run out of the state. They abolished football.

By 1905, USC had played twelve seasons of football. While the
sport's popularity continued to grow among students and alumni,
national public opinion against it swelled because of its brutal
nature that resulted in the deaths of several players across the
country. In 1905 alone, eighteen young men died from football-
related causes. President Theodore Roosevelt got into the act, telling the football-playing schools that they had better clean up the
game or he would have it abolished.

In Columbia, the trustees surrendered to public opinion and
abolished football at the university in 1906. The university's student newspaper, *The Gamecock*, wasn't too happy with the idea.
"It gives us pain to chronicle the season of 1906," the paper wrote.
"There was one ineradicable blot on the field of athletic possibil-
ities: the absence of football. An all-wise and overpowering Board
of Trustees decreed that ping-pong and croquet were better suited
for the physical upbuilding of our students."

GAMECOCKS

Not at pleased with the decision either, the students protested the absence of football until the board again relented. Halfway through what would have been the 1907 season, they reinstated football at USC. After a squad and a short schedule were hastily assembled, the Gamecocks beat Charleston, Georgia College, and The Citadel for a perfect 3-0 record.

Thanks to a bad idea, though, the year-by-year results of USC football note briefly "1906: Trustees Abolished Football."

That sure-fire investment you made from a pal's hot stock tip. The expensive exercise machine that now traps dust bunnies under your bed. Blond hair. Telling your wife you wanted to eat at the restaurant with the waitresses in little shorts. They seemed like pretty good ideas at the time; they weren't.

We all have bad ideas in our lifetime. They provide some of our most crucial learning experiences. Some ideas, though, are so irreparably and inherently bad that we cannot help but wonder why they were even conceived in the first place.

Almost two thousand years ago a man had just such an idea. Judas' betrayal of Jesus remains to this day one of the most heinous acts of treachery in history. Turning his back on Jesus was a bad idea for Judas then; it's a bad idea for us now.

Bat Day seems like a good idea, but I question the advisability of giving bats in the Bronx to 40,000 Yankee fans.

— Cartoonist Aaron Bacall

**We all have some pretty bad ideas
during our lifetimes, but nothing equals the folly
of turning away from Jesus.**

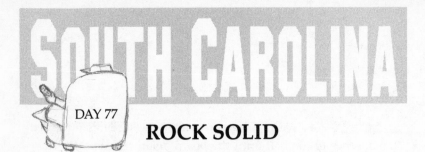

DAY 77

ROCK SOLID

Read Luke 6:46-49.

"I will show you what he is like who comes to me and hears my words and puts them into practice. He is like a man building a house, who dug down deep and laid the foundation on rock" (vv. 47-48).

They laid the foundation for "a time when every day was a holiday and every meal a feast in the world of Carolina basketball." They were the Four Horsemen and the Kid, and in the space of five nights in 1968 they showed the world what South Carolina basketball could be.

Jack Thompson, Skip Harlicka, and Frank Standard were in Frank McGuire's first recruiting class. Gary Gregor was sidelined with a knee injury when they arrived. The Kid – Bobby Cremins – followed two seasons later.

McGuire credited the 1965 team with laying the foundation for the appropriations for the Carolina Coliseum. In the "relic of a homecourt gym" that was the Carolina Fieldhouse, the Gamecocks whipped third-ranked Duke 73-71. "The Field House turned into a sea of frenzy" as many of the 3,200 jammed into the shoebox stormed the court "to celebrate the first step into the future." Everything changed with that magic night as now demand for tickets would outweigh supply.

But it was in 1968 that this bunch – four seniors and a sophomore – "showed that the Gamecocks could earn a seat at college basketball's head table." They laid the foundation for a decade of excellence under McGuire when in the space of five nights they beat Duke and North Carolina – both nationally ranked and on winning streaks -- on their home courts.

"That was a great time to be at South Carolina," Gregor said about that season when a "gang set the table and demonstrated what could be." They laid the foundation for greatness to follow.

Like USC's entire athletics program, your life is an ongoing project, a work in progress. As with any complex construction job, if your life is to be stable, it must have a solid foundation, which holds everything up and keeps everything together.

R. Alan Culpepper said in *The New Interpreter's Bible*, "We do not choose whether we will face severe storms in life; we only get to choose the foundation on which we will stand." In other words, tough times are inevitable. If your foundation isn't rock-solid, you will have nothing on which to stand as those storms buffet you, nothing to keep your life from flying apart into a cycle of disappointment and destruction.

But when the foundation is solid and sure, you can take the blows, stand strong, recover, and live with joy and hope. Only one foundation is sure and foolproof: Jesus Christ. Everything else you build upon will fail you.

Jesus Christ is the rock upon which I stand.
-- Heisman Trophy winner Danny Wuerffel

In the building of your life, you must start
with a foundation in Jesus Christ, or the first
trouble that shows up will knock you down.

SOUTH CAROLINA

DAY 78

TOP SECRET

Read Romans 2:1-16.

"This will take place on the day when God will judge men's secrets through Jesus Christ, as my gospel declares" (v. 16).

Warren Giese was convinced spies lurked in the scoreboard.

Giese was South Carolina's head football coach from 1956-'60. His approach to offense was so conservative that his teams rarely threw a pass. In 1957, for instance, Julius Derrick led the team in receiving with six catches. Alex Hawkins, a halfback and not a quarterback, was the team's leading passer that season when he completed nine of twelve attempts.

Giese said he preferred the 20-play, 80-yard drive that took ten minutes because "the other team can't score if it doesn't have the football." In defending his conservative approach to reporters, he employed NCAA statistics that revealed that most of the passing leaders had losing records.

After the two-point conversion was instituted in 1958, Giese used other statistics to support his unusual approach of always going for two. That philosophy created a unique situation in that his teams had no experienced place kickers. As a result, the Game-cocks did not attempt a single field goal during Giese's tenure.

Giese held closed practices that barred all outsiders, including the news media. He had the sports editor of *The State* thrown out of his first practice session. He used the Columbia minor league baseball park to practice in before the Clemson game because its high wooden fences afforded more security than did the usual practice fields. Once Giese noticed some movement in the scoreboard; convinced his practice was being spied on, he sent some security guards to check it out.

They surprised an amorous couple who had mistakenly thought they had found a place where they could be alone.

As Warren Giese was about his football practices, we have to be vigilant about the personal information we prefer to keep secret. Much information about us—from credit reports to what movies we rent—is readily available to prying and persistent persons. In our information age, people we don't know may know a lot about us—or at least they can find out. And some of them may use this information for harm.

While diligence may allow us to be reasonably successful in keeping some secrets from the world at large, we should never deceive ourselves into believing we are keeping secrets from God. God knows everything about us, including the things we wouldn't want proclaimed at church. All our sins, mistakes, failures, shortcomings, quirks, prejudices, and desires – God knows all our would-be secrets.

But here's something God hasn't kept a secret: No matter what he knows about us, he loves us still.

The secret of winning is working more as a team, less as individuals.
– Knute Rockne

We have no secrets before God, and it's no secret
that he nevertheless loves us still.

DAY 79

THE FAME GAME

Read 1 Kings 10:1-10, 18-29.

"King Solomon was greater in riches and wisdom than all the other kings of the earth. The whole world sought audience with Solomon" (vv. 23-24).

He was so unknown his name was misspelled in the 1999 media guide, but one play ensured his place in Gamecock football lore.

Erik Kimrey came to Columbia as a walk-on quarterback in 1998. He didn't rate a biography in the 1999 media guide, drawing a mention as a "squad member." His first name was incorrectly spelled "Eric." His complete entry in the 2000 media guide read "1999: Squad member. 1998: Squad member who was redshirted."

Kimrey did not play a single down in 1998 or 1999. USC had seven quarterbacks listed on the 1999 roster. Six of them played during the season; Kimrey was the seventh. He finally saw some action when he played sparingly in the first three games of 2000. His career totals thus read four completions in eight attempts with one interception, all against New Mexico State.

But then came the Mississippi State game. The Gamecocks trailed the Bulldogs 19-13 late in the fourth quarter. On third and ten from the State 25, quarterback Phil Petty was knocked down and suffered a sprained ankle. Coach Lou Holtz called on Kimrey to go in. "Coach, I can throw the fade route," Kimrey said. "When a player tells me he can do something, I'm all for that," Holtz later said. He called the fade. Receiver Jermale Kelly ran the route, and

Kimrey lofted a strike for a game-winning touchdown.

Kimrey was an immediate celebrity. National radio networks, *Sports Illustrated*, and local TV crews interviewed him, giving him his fifteen minutes of fame and forever ensuring that he became part of Gamecock football legend.

Have you ever wanted to be famous? Hanging out with other rich and famous people, having folks with microphones listen to what you say, throwing money around like toilet paper, meeting adoring and clamoring fans, signing autographs, and posing for the paparazzi before you climb into your imported sports car?

Many of us yearn to be famous, well-known in the places and by the people that we believe matter. That's all fame amounts to: strangers knowing your name and your face.

The truth is that you are already famous where it really does matter, which excludes TV's talking heads, screaming teenagers, moviegoers, or D.C. power brokers. You are famous because Almighty God knows your name, your face, and everything else there is to know about you.

If a persistent photographer snapped you pondering this fame – the only kind that has eternal significance – would the picture show the world unbridled joy or the shell-shocked expression of a mug shot?

Brother, that was big time.
– Nose tackle Cleveland Pinckney to Erik Kimrey

You're already famous because God knows
your name and your face, which may be either
reassuring or terrifying.

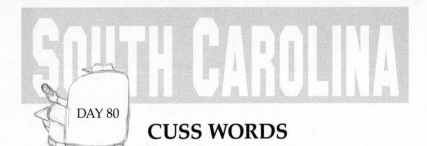

DAY 80

CUSS WORDS

Read Psalm 10.

"[The wicked man's] mouth is full of curses and lies and threats; trouble and evil are under his tongue" (v. 7).

Deeply religious and a man of character and conviction, Bobby Richardson once almost cussed during a disagreement with an umpire while he was head coach of the Gamecock baseball team.

When Athletic Director Paul Dietzel hired Richardson in 1969, the move was not a sure thing. Though he was described as "a folk hero" in South Carolina, Richardson had no experience as a coach or a recruiter.

Richardson was a star second baseman for the New York Yankees for 11 seasons. He won five Gold Gloves; in 1962 he finished second in the league MVP voting behind Mickey Mantle.

Dietzel promised Richardson an increase in budget and some improvement in facilities. Baseball had long been a low priority at South Carolina with only part-time coaches that included "a football assistant, a physical education professor, [and] a professor of English." Collegiate baseball powers typically played 50 to 60 games a season; South Carolina had never scheduled 35.

Richardson had a losing first year in 1970, but that was the last one South Carolina would have for 26 seasons. In 1974, the Gamecocks finished 48-8 and received their first-ever bid to the NCAA playoffs. His 1975 team went 51-6-1 and went all the way to the College World Series championship game before losing to

Texas. In seven seasons, his record was 220-91-2.

About that time Richardson almost cussed. Tom Price tells the story that in a game against Davidson in 1970, Richardson came out to question a particularly heinous call. Apparently having a bad day, the umpire threatened to throw Richardson out of the game unless he immediately returned to the dugout. Price wrote, "Just as Richardson reached the dugout, he turned, pointed at the umpire, and said, 'Phooey on you.'"

We live in a coarsened culture where words no one would utter in polite society a few decades ago now spew from our music and our television sets—and our own mouths. Honestly answer these indelicate questions: With what name did you christen that slow driver you couldn't pass? What unflattering words did you have for that stubborn golf ball that wouldn't stay in the fairway? And what four-letter words do you sprinkle liberally in your conversations with people whom you want to think of you as "cool"?

Some argue that profane language is really harmless expression. It is in reality quite damaging, though, because of what its use reveals about the speaker: a lack of character, a lack of vocabulary, and a lack of respect for others and reverence for God.

The words we speak reveal what's in our heart, and what God seeks there is love and gentleness, not vileness.

American professional athletes are bilingual; they speak English and profanity.

-- NHL Legend Gordie Howe

**Our words -- including profane ones --
expose what's in our hearts.**

DAY 81

GOOD SPORTS

Read Titus 2:1-8.

"Show integrity, seriousness and soundness of speech that cannot be condemned, so that those who oppose you may be ashamed because they have nothing bad to say about us" (vv. 7b, 8).

Upset by a show of poor sportsmanship, USC track legend Bob Crombie "riled the Clemson faithful in a moment that will live forever in Carolina lore."

Crombie arrived in Columbia in 1963 from Australia after drawing the interest of track and field coach Weems Baskin with a letter inquiring about scholarships. At USC, Crombie never lost a race in his specialty, the half-mile, at home, in the state meet, or in the ACC championships.

Because NCAA rules limited athletes from other countries to two seasons of competition, Crombie ran for USC in 1964 and '65 only. "I regret that the international athletes rule prevented me from competing my senior year," Crombie said. "I was ready to do something really special."

He was special enough to be inducted into USC's Athletic Hall of Fame in 2006 -- and to get back at Clemson's fans in a legendary way. At a meet at Clemson, Crombie "took exception at attempts by the Tigers' fans to upset USC triple-jumper J.R. Wilburn. 'Poor sportsmanship,'" Crombie said. He then "dusted the field in the 800 as usual," but instead of his normal finish, "he ran the last few yards [of the race] backward and blew kisses to the crowd."

Neither the Clemson fans nor athletes appreciated his gesture. When a Tiger pushed Crombie, he pushed back. Some fans rushed onto the track, and the team's throwers – the muscle men – served as bodyguards for Crombie. He always felt Baskin didn't really mind his showing up Clemson for its poor sportsmanship.

One of life's paradoxes is that many who would never consider cheating on the tennis court or the racquetball court or trying to rattle an opponent just to gain an advantage think nothing of doing so in other areas of their life. In other words, the good sportsmanship they practice on the golf course or even on the Monopoly board doesn't carry over. They play with the truth, cut corners, abuse others verbally, run roughshod over weaker people, and generally cheat whenever they can to gain an advantage on the job or in their personal relationships.

But good sportsmanship is a way of living, not just of playing. Shouldn't you accept defeat without complaint (You don't have to like it.); win gracefully without gloating; treat your competition with fairness, courtesy, generosity, and respect? That's the way one team treats another in the name of sportsmanship. That's the way one person treats another in the name of Jesus.

One person practicing sportsmanship is better than a hundred teaching it.

-- Knute Rockne

Sportsmanship -- treating others with courtesy, fairness, and respect -- is a way of living, not just a way of playing.

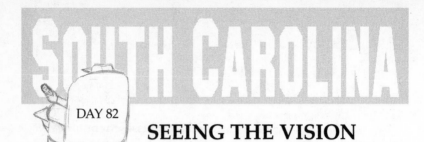
DAY 82

SEEING THE VISION

Read Acts 26:1, 9-23.

"So then, . . . I was not disobedient to the vision from heaven" (v. 19).

Paul Dietzel didn't deliver the top-ten rankings and big bowl games the Carolina faithful hoped for, but he was a visionary whose impact on USC athletics continues to be felt.

When Dietzel arrived in Columbia in 1966, "South Carolina's athletic facilities charitably could be called modest. By today's standards, they would be labeled primitive," said one writer.

The baseball team often played its homes games on a diamond at the Veterans Hospital. Master groundskeeper Sarge Frye trucked in cinders for the track and scrounged railroad ties for seating at the baseball field. The tennis program had no scholarships, and the university bulldozed the courts for an administration building. The tennis team moved to "clay" courts that were really dirt at Maxcy Gregg Park. "We just hoped too many rocks didn't come up," said Coach Don Barton.

And along came Dietzel, who "burst onto the Carolina scene . . . with a plan for the future." He "set about thrusting the Gamecocks to a place among the nation's best." When he saw Carolina Stadium -- a wooden arena built during the Depression that seated 43,000 -- he knew what his first project was. "My first thought was, 'Get that stadium improved,'" Dietzel said.

And he did with an expansion and renovation completed in

1972, along with the building of the Roost, new tennis courts, Carolina Coliseum, lights and new seating at the baseball field, and the George Terry Spring Sports Building.

Paul Dietzel was "a leader, a builder, . . . and the catalyst" who charged South Carolina into the future, said USC sports historian Tom Price. Gamecock athletic administrator John Moore called Dietzel "a real visionary."

To speak of visions is often to risk their being lumped with palm readings, Ouija boards, seances, horoscopes, and other such useless mumbo-jumbo. The danger such mild amusements pose, however, is very real in that they indicate a reliance on something other than God. It is God who knows the future; it is God who has a vision and a plan for your life; it is God who has the answers you seek as you struggle to find your way.

You probably do have a vision for your life, a plan for how it should unfold. It's the dream you pursue through your family, your job, your hobbies, your interests.

But your vision inspires a fruitful life only if it is compatible with God's plan. As the apostle Paul found out, you ignore God's vision at your peril. But if you pursue it, you'll find an even more glorious life than you could ever have envisioned for yourself.

If I could see into the future, I wouldn't be sitting here talking to you doorknobs. I'd be out investing in the stock market.
-- Boston Celtic Kevin McHale to reporters

Your grandest vision for the future pales beside the vision God has of what the two of you can accomplish together.

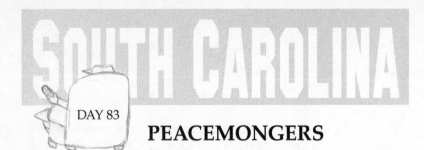

DAY 83

PEACEMONGERS

Read Hebrews 12:14-17.

"Make every effort to live in peace with all men and to be holy" (v. 14).

The intensity of the South Carolina-Clemson rivalry threatened to erupt in violence and bloodshed in the Riot of 1902.

The Gamecocks beat Clemson 12-6 on Big Thursday, Oct. 30, getting two touchdowns from Guy Gunter. As always, the Clemson cadets remained in Columbia after the game to enjoy the State Fair. A downtown merchant hung a big transparency in his store window "depicting a gamecock crowing over a bedraggled-looking tiger." Insulted by the sketch, the Clemson men warned the Columbia students they better not show up with the thing at the Elks parade the next day. That's all it took, of course, to ensure the gloating gamecock's presence.

Following the parade, the Clemson students, armed with bayonets and swords, marched to the Sumter Street campus entrance where "a small band of Carolina students crouched behind hastily arranged defenses at the old wall." They were reportedly armed with "pistols, sticks, bricks, and anything else resembling a weapon." A senior called out to USC freshman Rion McKissick, who would later become president of the university, "McKissick, are you armed?" McKissick showed him a revolver, whereupon the senior ordered him, "Make every shot count."

Before blood could be shed, though, Christie Benet, a member of the Carolina teams of 1897 and 1898, showed up and offered to "take on any two Clemson students in hand-to-hand combat" to resolve the dispute. That didn't work, but he managed to stall until police and school officials arrived. A committee of six students worked out a compromise that included the burning of the controversial transparency while the two student bodies cheered.

Perhaps you've never been in a brawl or a public brouhaha to match that of the Riot of 1902, but maybe you retaliated when you got one elbow too many in a pickup basketball game. Or maybe you and your spouse or your teenager get into it occasionally, shouting and saying cruel things. Or road rage may be a part of your life.

While we do seem to live in a more belligerent, confrontational society than ever before, fighting is still not the solution to a problem. Rather, it only escalates the whole confrontation, leaving wounded pride, intransigence, and simmering hatred in its wake. Actively seeking and making peace is the way to a solution that lasts and heals.

Peacemaking as Christie Benet did is not as easy as fighting, but it is much more courageous and a lot less painful. It is also the Jesus thing to do.

No matter what the other fellow does on the field, don't let him lure you into a fight. Uphold your dignity.
-- Alabama Coach Frank Thomas

Making peace instead of fighting takes courage and strength; it's also what Jesus would do.

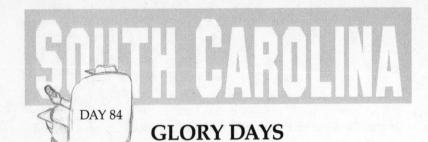

SOUTH CAROLINA

DAY 84

GLORY DAYS

Read Colossians 3:1-4.

"When Christ, who is your life, appears, then you also will appear with him in glory" (v. 4).

Travis Kraft didn't play a whole lot of basketball for the Gamecocks, but he had his moment of glory.

Kraft came to Columbia from North Dakota in 1999 with a reputation as an outstanding three-point shooter. A stress fracture hobbled him his freshman season, and he averaged only 3.8 points per game.

Another leg injury put him on the bench for the early part of the 2000-01 season. When fifth-ranked Florida came to Carolina Coliseum on Jan. 7, Kraft had played only 32 minutes all season and had scored only seven points. As he expected, he spent the whole first half on the bench. Still, Coach Eddie Fogler told him at halftime, "Be ready; we may need you."

Florida led 63-53 with less than five minutes to play when Carolina's pressing defense began to take its toll. Kraft entered the game for the first time with 19 seconds left but played only a fraction more than two seconds. He returned with 11.5 seconds left. Florida led by two when the Gamecocks got the ball out of bounds with 2.5 seconds on the clock. Kraft was about to enjoy his moment of Gamecock glory.

He inbounded the ball to Calvin Clemmons. Closely guarded, Clemmons flipped the ball back to Kraft, who launched a 25-

footer. It hit nothing but net as the buzzer blared, and USC won 69-68. Kraft, who played a total of 13.7 seconds, was mobbed and pummeled to the floor by exuberant teammates.

You may well remember the play that was your moment of athletic glory. Or the night you received an award from a civic group for your hard work. Your first (and last?) ace on the golf course. Your promotion at work. Your first-ever 10K race. Life does have its moments of glory.

But they are a lesser, transient glory, which actually bears pain with it since you cannot recapture the moment. The excitement, the joy, even the happiness – they are fleeting; they pass as quickly as they arose, and you can never experience them again.

Glory days that last forever are found only through Jesus. That's because true glory properly belongs only to God, who has shown us his glory in Jesus. To accept Jesus into our lives is thus to take God's glory into ourselves. Glory therefore is an ongoing attribute of Christians. Our glory days are right now, and they will become even more glorious when Jesus returns.

Travis Kraft's foot injury flared up again after his moment of glory against Florida, and he didn't play another second in 2001. He then left school.

The real glory is being knocked to your knees and then coming back. That's real glory. That's the essence of it.

-- Vince Lombardi

The glory of this earth is fleeting, but the glory we find in Jesus lasts forever – and will only get even more magnificent.

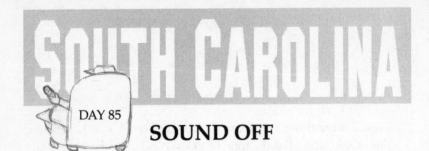
DAY 85

SOUND OFF

Read Revelation 4:1-10, 5:6-14.

"Then I looked and heard the voice of many angels, numbering thousands upon thousands, and ten thousand times ten thousand" (v. 11a).

Thump. Thump. In the quiet of a largely silent crowd, they rang loud and clear. And they were sweet music to Gamecock ears.

USC was 3-1 for the season when Mississippi State breezed into town on Sept. 29, 2007. The Gamecock crowd was raucous as they filed into the stadium. After all, this was a sure win.

The crowd turned eerily silent in the third quarter, though, when the Bulldogs drove it right down the Gamecocks' throats to take the lead. USC then missed a field goal, and an apprehensive crowd sat on its hands watching the season slip away.

Or so it thought.

That's when the two thumps showed up and turned the game around. The first thump was the sound of toe meeting leather: State punting the football. The second thump was the sound of body meeting leather: Eric Norwood blocking the punt. "Once I freed the center, nobody came to pick me up," Norwood said. "We thought we could block one, and we did."

"In the twinkling of an eye, the Bulldogs went from in control to in retreat. . . . The blocked punt brought [special teams coach Shane] Beamer onto the field to lead the cheers, and suddenly bolts of electricity ricocheted through the arena." The crowd

GAMECOCKS

came to life and so did the Gamecocks. On the first play after the block, Chris Smelley hit Kenny McKinley with a touchdown pass. The Gamecocks were on their way to a 38-21 win.

"We can finally say special teams won a game now," Coach Steve Spurrier said.

And they made a lot of noise in the process.

Williams-Brice Stadium erupts in a cacophony on game day. Loud music blares from the rattling speakers in the car next to you at the traffic light. The garbage men bang the cans around as though they earn bonuses for waking you up. A silence of any length in a conversation makes us uncomfortable; somebody please say something.

We live in a noisy world, which means activity, busyness, progress, and engagement with life. The problem with all that noise – however constructive it may be – is that it drowns out God's gentle voice. Thus, some quiet time each day is absolutely imperative if we are to grow our relationship with God. The intentional seeking of silence in which to hear God's voice constitutes surrender to the divine.

Accustomed to noise as we are, we will be quite comfortable in Heaven. Revelation's lengthy description of God's home makes it very clear that it's a noisy place reverberating with the inspiring, exhilarating, and awesome sound of worship.

You can tell a good putt by the noise it makes.
-- Pro Hall of Fame golfer Bobby Locke

Heaven is a quite noisy place, echoing constantly with the wonderful sounds of worship.

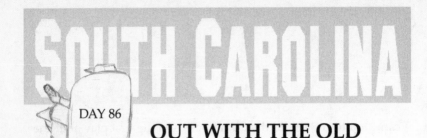

DAY 86

OUT WITH THE OLD

Read Hebrews 8:3-13.

"The ministry Jesus has received is as superior to theirs as the covenant of which he is mediator is superior to the old one, and it is founded on better promises" (v. 6).

The modern era of women's basketball at South Carolina began in 1974, but the ladies actually played roundball in Columbia more than fifty years before that.

Women's sports were called "Co-Ed Athletics" when they first began at USC. In 1923, the co-ed basketball team – nicknamed the "Pullets" -- competed against other schools such as Newberry and the College of Charleston. They had a 7-6 record in 1923 and raised some eyebrows by taking a road trip to Charleston.

In 1925, for the first time, the Pullets wore regular basketball uniforms complete with numerals similar to those worn by the men's team. They also became the first women's team in the state to make out-of-state road trips. That 1925 squad compiled a 5-7 record, and their road trips included a groundbreaking five-game, five-day trip to Virginia to play women's basketball teams at Fredericksburg, Westhampton, Farmville, and William & Mary.

Intercollegiate women's basketball was no longer allowed in the 1930s. Instead, under the auspices of the Women's Athletic Association, the women were divided by their classes (e.g., sophomores and juniors) and played against each other in the beginnings of the intramural programs still offered today.

GAMECOCKS

In 1967, women's basketball began competing as a club team without a budget or uniforms, playing other college club squads across the state. In 1973, the club team appeared in the Carolina Coliseum for the first time as preliminaries for the men's game. The doubleheaders were a huge success with the fans, and the USC Athletics Department took over the women's club team.

The new, modern era of women's basketball at USC had begun, the old way of doing things discarded forever.

Your car's running fine, but the miles are adding up; time for a trade-in. Your TV's still delivering a sharp picture, but, man, those HDTV's are really something. Same with the newer, faster computers. And how about those lawn mowers that turn on a dime?

Out with the old, in with the new — we're always looking for the newest thing on the market. In our faith life, that means the new covenant God gave us through Jesus Christ. An old covenant did exist, one based on the law God handed down to the Hebrew people. But God used this old covenant as the basis to go one better and establish a covenant available to the whole world. This new way is a covenant of grace between God and anyone who lives a life of faith in Jesus.

Don't get caught waiting for a newer, improved covenant; the promises God gave us through Jesus couldn't get any better.

The old ballplayer cared about the name on the front [of the jersey]. The new ballplayer cares about the name on the back.
— Former major leaguer Steve Garvey

**It just doesn't get any better
than God's new covenant in Jesus Christ.**

SOUTH CAROLINA

DAY 87

A HOLLYWOOD ENDING

Read Luke 24:1-12.

"Why do you look for the living among the dead? He is not here; he has risen!" (vv. 5, 6a)

Pitch this to a Hollywood script writer.

School says you're too slow and too small to play for us, son. So he goes to another school. Player gets hurt so he gets to start bowl game – against that team that spurned him. He is MVP.

Too hokey even for the movies? Maybe so -- but it's the true story of Ryan Brewer.

Brewer grew up an Ohio State fan, but the Buckeyes wouldn't give him the time of day, so he came south to Columbia. As a sophomore in 2000, he played wide receiver. The team's best player undoubtedly was running back Derek Watson, who led the SEC in all-purpose yards. The Gamecocks went 7-4 in Lou Holtz's second season and accepted a bid to the Outback Bowl to play – guess who? -- Ohio State.

The Hollywood story really began to unfold when Holtz suspended Watson for the bowl game for violating team rules. Brewer had played tailback in high school and as a freshman in Columbia. He had carried the ball only 14 times during the 2000 season but was Holtz's choice to replace Watson.

In real life, he probably gets stuffed and Ohio State wins easily. But this is Hollywood, remember? Or is it? All Brewer did was rush for 109 yards in 19 carries, catch three passes for 92 yards, return two punts for 18 yards – that's 219 total yards – and score all three touchdowns as the Gamecocks whipped Ohio State 24-7. Not surprisingly, Brewer was a unanimous choice for the game's Most Valuable Player.

"I never dreamed anything like this would happen," Brewer said. Hey, this is Hollywood, kid.

The world tells us that happy endings are for fairy tales and the movies, that reality is Cinderella dying in childbirth and her prince getting killed in a peasant uprising. But that's just another of the world's lies.

The truth is that Jesus Christ has been producing happy endings for almost two millennia. That's because in Jesus lies the power to change and to rescue a life no matter how desperate the situation. Jesus is the master at putting shattered lives back together, of healing broken hearts and broken relationships, of resurrecting lost dreams.

And as for living happily ever after – God really means it. The greatest Hollywood ending of them all was written on a Sunday morning centuries ago when Jesus left a tomb and death behind. With faith in Jesus, your life can have that same ending. You live with God in peace, joy, and love – forever. The End.

You're not here to prove anything to anybody at Ohio State. You're here to help your teammates.
-- Lou Holtz to Ryan Brewer before the Outback Bowl

Hollywood's happy endings are products of imagination; the happy endings Jesus produces are real and are yours for the asking.

DAY 88

TEAM PLAYERS

Read 1 Corinthians 12:4-13; 27-31.

"Now to each one the manifestation of the Spirit is given for the common good" (v. 7).

South Carolina's first-ever NCAA national championship was such a team effort that the Gamecocks clinched the title in an event they didn't even win.

In June 2002, the South Carolina women's track and field team won the NCAA Outdoor Track and Field title in Baton Rouge, the school's first-ever NCAA team title in any sport.

As time neared for the 200-meter dash, the final event on the final day, Gamecock Coach Curtis Frye did the math. Only UCLA had a chance at snatching the national championship away from USC. So he told his runners, Aleen Bailey and Lisa Barber, they needed to come up with six points. With that in mind and all that pressure on their shoulders, Bailey finished second and Barber finished fifth. That was good enough for twelve points; USC topped UCLA 82-72 for the championship. "I am so happy to finish second," Bailey said. "I know the points helped the team."

Only an hour before the 200-meter finals, the Gamecocks had put themselves in great shape by collecting 19 points in the 400-meter dash when Barber, Lashinda Demus, and Demetria Washington finished second, third, and fourth respectively. Earlier that day, the 4x400-meter relay team of Tiffany Ross, Washington, Tacita Bass, and Demus set an NCAA championship and collegiate record.

"I am so proud of our entire team," Barber said. "I think our kids understand what it means to be a class act and win a championship," an ecstatic Frye said. "I have waited 27 years for this."

For his team to win a national championship.

Most accomplishments are the result of teamwork, whether it's a college track and field team, the running of a household, or the completion of a project at work. Disparate talents and gifts work together for the common good and the greater goal.

A church works exactly the same way. At its most basic, a church is a team that has been and is being assembled by God. A shared faith drives the team members and impels them toward shared goals. As a successful Gamecock track and field team must have sprinters, jumpers, and throwers, so must a church be composed of people with different spiritual and personal gifts. The result is something greater than everyone involved.

What makes a church team different from others is that the individual efforts are expended for the glory of God and not for self. The nature of a church member's particular talents doesn't matter; what does matter is that those talents are used as part of God's team.

Money may be the most important element in modern-day stock car racing, but team chemistry runs a very close second.
– NASCAR's Bill Elliott

A church is a team of people
using their various talents and gifts for God,
the source of all those abilities to begin with.

DAY 89

PRECIOUS MEMORIES

Read 1 Corinthians 11:23-26.

"Do this in remembrance of me" (v. 24b).

When asked in 1995 how he expected to be remembered by the Gamecock faithful, Steve Taneyhill replied, "That crazy Yankee quarterback." Most likely he is remembered today as the boisterous, pony-tailed quarterback who delivered a legendary insult to the Clemson Tigers.

Sports Illustrated said Taneyhill's hair hung "from the back of his football helmet like a mud flap." Hair and all, he exploded onto the Gamecock Nation after an 0-5 start to the 1992 season when Coach Sparky Woods turned to the 18-year-old freshman in desperation. He led South Carolina to wins over No. 15 Mississippi State and No. 16 Tennessee.

It was in the last game of that 1992 season, however, that Taneyhill made an indelible impression upon Gamecock fans, and not just because he led South Carolina to a 24-13 win. The Gamecocks led 17-13 in the fourth quarter when Brandon Bennett broke loose for a long run that set up the clinching touchdown. Taneyhill was jogging downfield to catch up to the play when he crossed the Tiger paw in the middle of the field. Confident that the Gamecocks had Clemson beat, he impulsively knelt down and pretended to sign it. "At that time, I thought nothing of it. I just thought it was funny," Taneyhill said. "But obviously it turned into something way bigger than that because I still hear about it today."

School records for completions, touchdown passes, career completion percentage and second only to Todd Ellis for career passing yards – and Steve Taneyhill may still be best remembered for signing his name on the dotted paw.

As is Steve Taneyhill's fabulous career at Columbia, your whole life will one day be only a memory because – hold your breath for this red-hot news flash -- you will die.

You can plan for that momentous day by selecting a funeral home, purchasing a cemetery plot and picking out your casket or opting for cremation and choosing a tasteful urn, designating those who will deliver your eulogy, and even making other less important decisions about your send-off.

What you cannot control about your death, however, is how you will be remembered and whether your demise leaves a gaping hole in the lives of those with whom you shared your life or a pothole that's quickly paved over. What determines whether those nice words someone will say about you are heartfelt truth or pleasant fabrications? What determines whether the tears that fall at your death result from heartfelt grief or a sinus infection?

Love does. The love you give away during your life decides how you will be remembered at your death.

I don't want my children to remember me as a professional football player. I want them to remember me as a man of God.
– Reggie White

How you will be remembered after you die
is largely determined by how much
and how deeply you love others now.

DAY 90

THE HEALING TOUCH

Read Matthew 17:14-20.

"If you have faith as small as a mustard seed, you can say to this mountain, 'Move from here to there' and it will move. Nothing will be impossible for you" (v. 20).

Tre Kelley was seriously injured, so he turned to God for healing.

Kelley was a three-year starter at guard for the Gamecocks (2004-07). He was All-SEC as a junior and a senior and was the team MVP as a senior. Thus, the news was devastating to the team in January 2007 when "the one man the Gamecocks could absolutely not do without" suffered a knee injury that would require surgery and sideline him for at least a month.

But Kelley had a different take on the injury. He relied on God and not man to heal him. "I told the trainers, I told the doctors, and I told coach I'm fine," he said. "I want to be out there to help my basketball team, so put me out there. I don't want surgery. I want to go out there and play."

After his freshman year in 2004, while he was on a basketball mission trip to the Dominican Republic, Kelley accepted Christ. He said at the time, "God had a plan to make me a stronger and better person." And in 2007 he prayed that God would indeed make him a stronger person by healing him and letting him play against 8th-ranked Kansas a week after the injury.

So what happened? Kelley started and played virtually the

entire game. "My knee feels great," he said after the game. "I don't know if [God] (completely) healed it yet, but He made it possible for me to go out there and play." "The good Lord is working on him. It's amazing," Coach Dave Odom commented.

The good Lord indeed used Tre Kelley's faith and the power of prayer to heal him in a way that by all medical standards was a miracle.

If we believe in miraculous healing at all, we have pretty much come to consider it to be a relatively rare occurrence. All too often, our initial reaction when we are ill or hurting is to call a doctor rather than to pray. Tre Kelley's total reliance on God is not necessarily our approach. If we really want to move a mountain, we'll round up some heavy-duty earthmoving equipment.

The truth is, though, that divine healing occurs with quite astonishing regularity; the problem is our perspective. We are usually quite effusive in our thanks to and praise for a doctor or a particular medicine without considering that God is the one who is responsible for all healing.

We should remember also that "natural" healing occurs because our bodies react as God created them to. Those healings, too, are divine; they, too, are miraculous. Faith healing is really nothing more – or less – than giving credit where credit is due.

God definitely answered my prayers and enabled me to come back and play.

-- Tre Kelley

**God does in fact heal continuously everywhere;
all too often we just don't notice.**

NOTES
(by Devotion Day Number)

1   In October 1891, Furman University . . . team of their own.: Kamon Simpson, *Gamecocks Handbook* (Wichita, KS: The Wichita Eagle and Beacon Publishing Co., 1996), p. 6.

1   The student body had voted . . . part of its holiday festivities.: Simpson, *Gamecocks Handbook*, p. 7.

1   The Carolina team was hastily . . . without faculty permission.": Jim Hunter, *The Gamecocks* (Huntsville, AL: The Strode Publishers, 1975), p. 14.

1   "Christmas Eve dawned bright . . . both teams to the site.: John Chandler Griffin, *The First Hundred Years* (Atlanta: Longstreet Press, 1992), p. 1.

1   Several hundred fans paid fifty cents each: Simpson, *Gamecocks Handbook*, p. 7.

1   "the boys boarded the train . . . still in the ring.": Hunter, p. 14.

2   "Suggs rolled to his right . . . with just 4:54 left to play.": Simpson, *Gamecocks Handbook*, p. 60.

2   South Carolina scored 29 points in 10:01: Tom Price, *Tales from the Gamecocks' Roost* (Champaign, IL: Sports Publishing, LLC, 2002), p. 63.

3   Buzzer-beaters are the salsa . . . or the final record, is forgotten,": Bob Gillespie, "Beating the Clock," *The State*, Jan 9, 2001, http://docs.newsbank.com/s/InfoWeb/aggdocs/NewsBank/0F0F75D58B693A40, May 6, 2009.

3   "I can do it," he told coach Eddie Fogler right before he did it.: Gillespie, "Beating the Clock."

3   "I've got knots on my . . . jumping all over me,": Gillespie, "Beating the Clock."

3   6-3 guard Kevin Joyce controlled . . . I got a piece of it,": Gillespie, "Beating the Clock."

3   "I've had none finer.": Gillespie, "Beating the Clock."

4   Petty knew the offense had been . . . things but didn't convert.": Rick Scoppe and Charlie Bennett, *Game of My Life: South Carolina* (Champaign, IL: Sports Publishing L.L.C., 2007), p. 172.

4   So Petty got his guys together . . . enough to win the game.": Scoppe and Bennett, p. 173.

4   Petty knew he could find . . . and converted the touchdown.": Scoppe and Bennett, p. 173.

4   Never let your mouth . . . your body can't cash.: *Price, Tales from the Gamecocks' Roost*, p. 97.

5   The championship trophy – a replica . . . Scott is relatively responsible,": Joseph Person, "Road Trip," *The State*, Jan. 6, 2007, http://docs.newsbank.com/s/InfoWeb/aggdocs/NewsBank/1168D4A68E823008, May 7, 2009.

6   Those are the differing . . . mirror in the morning.: Ron Morris, "Berson Happy to Be USC's One and Only," *The State*, Sept. 30, 2005, http://docs.newsbank.com/s/InfoWeb/aggdocs/NewsBank/10CF8F2A418D00D0, May 6, 2009.

6   "At least I know I'm right . . . the program could really be.: Morris, "Berson Happy."

6   "recruited the players, scheduled . . . cemetery on the other end.": Morris, "Berson Happy."

6   from looking in the mirror during . . . fast approaching legendary status.": Morris, "Berson Happy."

7   "Plain and simple, Spurrier . . . virtually void of direction.": Ron Morris, "Forget the Ending, This Season Was a Success," *The State*, Jan. 1, 2006, http://docs.newsbank.com/s/InfoWeb/aggdocs/NewsBank/10EE396E0DC033E0, May 7, 2009.

7   He dismissed about a dozen . . . "Beat Clemson" signs came down.: Morris, "Forget the Ending."

8   With 46 seconds left in the . . . with only 3:07 left.: Simpson, *Gamecocks Handbook*, p. 90.

8   scored from the one on a quarterback keeper with only 54 seconds left.: Simpson, *Gamecocks Handbook*, p. 90.

8   Hagler's last extra point had tied the school record of 42 straight.: Simpson, *Gamecocks Handbook*, pp. 90, 92.

8   Hagler missed the kick, . . . twelve men on the field.: Simpson, *Gamecocks Handbook*, p. 92.

9   Randy Martz had the makings . . . never gave baseball a shot.: Price, *Tales from the Gamecocks' Roost*, p. 140.

9   Before the 1977 baseball season . . . because he's no athlete.": Price, *Tales from the Gamecocks' Roost*, pp. 140-41.

9   He was named to every All-America team: Price, *Tales from the Gamecocks' Roost*, p. 141.

9   In both of his . . . left with the lead.: Price, *Tales from the Gamecocks' Roost*, p. 141.

10   He played for Clemson in 1942, . . . to report for football practice.: Griffin, p. 73.

10   When he explained his moral dilemma . . . play [his] heart out.": Griffin, p. 73.

10   One play included a line shift . . . about catching no passes.": Griffin, pp. 73-74.

11   Steve Taneyhill told his . . . we're going to score,": Scoppe and Bennett, p. 72.

11   "We don't have much time," . . . we got it, we got it,": Scoppe and Bennett, p. 72.

11   "Same play!": Price, *Tales from the Roost*, p. 123.

11   "went through the cadence. It was blocked perfectly.": Scoppe and Bennett, p. 72.

11   "they kind of stopped me . . . sure I got in there.": Scoppe and Bennett, p. 73.

12   This league is a bloodbath. That's what makes it so great.": Curry Kirkpatrick, "The Toughest Kid on Anybody's Block," *Sports Illustrated*, Jan. 4, 1972, http://vault.sportsillustrated.cnn.com/vault/article/magazine/MAG1084442/index.htm, April 21, 2009.

12   "snarling alley guy the . . . to call its own.": Kirkpatrick.

12   "the most revered name in Gamecock basketball history.": Gail Crouch, "Legendary John Roche Returns to Columbia," *Moore School of Business Alumni News*, July 26, 2007, http://mooreschoo.sc.edu/moore/pr/news/Alumni_News/roche_john_returns.html, April 21, 2009.

12   Roche was a "star ball handler with a textbook jump shot," Crouch.

12   He came to the gym the next night . . . an amazing hothead. Ask him.": Kirkpatrick.

13   In 2006, Natasha Hastings was ready . . . during the winter break.: Joseph Person, "Still on Track," *The State*, June 6, 2007, http://docs.newsbank.com/s/InfoWeb/aggdocs/NewsBank/1199E6E0D401F2C0, May 7, 2009.

14   The team improved as young men . . . fans of the two colleges.": Hunter, p. 102.

14   in Jacksonville, Fla., the Lions Club . . . Gamecocks as the host team: Hunter, p. 103.

14   a rematch of the Wake Forest game. . . . and never revived it.: Hunter, p. 104.

15   Near the end of the game, . . . at USC as a mama's boy.: Ron Morris, "Brawl Seals 'Momma's Boy' Label," *The State*, Feb. 22, 2008, http://docs.newsbank.com/s/InfoWeb/aggdocs/NewsBank/11F23F5A73B10C28, May 7, 2009.

15   One thing I refuse to do is live in fear.: Greg Garber, "At What Price Olympic Glory," *ESPN.com*, July 15, 2004.

16   Defensive coordinator Tom Gadd applied . . . getting after the football.": Price, *Tales from the Gamecocks' Roost*, p. 83.

17   Jones was an all-state basketball . . . started out as a manager: Joseph Person, "Moving on Up," *The State*, Dec. 22, 2007, http://docs.newsbank.com/s/InfoWeb/aggdocs/NewsBank/11E466F216592160, May 7, 2009.

18   Tom Price recounted Parone's adventures . . . won three state football championships: Price, *Tales from the Roost*, pp. 127-28.

19   Her marriage to the game . . . reinstated softball without missing a game.: Ron Morris, "USC Softball: Players Learn Value," *The State*, May 25, 2007, http://docs.newsbank.com/s/InfoWeb/aggdocs/NewsBank/1196EF4FA967AF88, May 7, 2009.

20   "What I learned in high school . . . and inner drive are remarkable.": Ron Aiken, "Athletes of the Past 20 Years: Duce Staley," *The State*, Sept. 20, 2001, http://docs.newsbank.com/s/InfoWeb/aggsdoc/NewsBank/0EEABC40C759A4C3, May 6, 2009.

21   I've been through hard times," . . . the whole rest of the season,".: Steve Wiseman, "Better Times," *The State*, May 30, 2003, http://docs.newsbank.com/s/InfoWeb/aggdocs/NewsBank/0FB61689FA794D8D, May 6, 2009.

21   "I'm elated with the season . . . a big key for us.": Wiseman, "Better Times."

22   who had little experience in the . . . the season opener against The Citadel,: Scoppe and Bennett, p. 120.

22   South Carolina scored with a . . . that's how I got started.": Scoppe and Bennett, p. 121.

23   "first sports idol," . . . and a matinee idol.": Ron Morris, "Steve Wadiak: The Heartbreak Kid," *GoGamecocks.com*, Nov. 2, 2008, http://www.thestate.com/gogamecocks/ronmorris/story/574995.html, April 21, 2009.

23   on the recommendation of a former player.: Hunter, p. 112.

23   "knock-down good-looking" . . . wore well on others.": Morris, "Steve Wadiak."

23   Wadiak shared playing time with Bishop Strickland in 1948,: Hunter, p. 113.

23   he "was branded forever as the greatest . . . surpassing Earl Clary,: Morris, "Steve Wadiak."

23   left the road at about 90 miles an hour.: Morris, "Steve Wadiak."

23   No one knows when he or she . . . in the blink of an eye.: Jim & Julie S. Bettinger, *The Book of Bowden* (Nashville, TN: TowleHouse Publishing, 2001), p. 21.

24   "They were up by a substantial . . . Elgin Baylor and Wilt Chamberlain.: Bob Spear, "Humble in the Wake of Greatness," *The State*, Feb. 1, 2003, http://docs.newsbank.com/s/InfoWeb/aggdocs/NewsBank/0F8F359206F6E7D7, May 6, 2009.

24   "I loved basketball," . . . I just wanted to play.": Spear, "Humble in the Wake."

25   In two years of feverish work, . . . construction of sewer lines.: Pat Butler, "Visionary Inventor Robinson Dies at 50," *The State*, April 13, 1998, http://docs.newsbank.com/s/InfoWeb/aggdocs/NewsBank/0EB587251CE41146, May 11, 2009.

25   which at the time were simply gutted steel boxes in need of a paint job: Wayne Drehs, "All Aboard!" *ESPN.com*, Oct 16, 2003, http://sports.espn.go.com/espn/print?id=1639333&type=page2Story, May 11, 2009.

25   "People would look at you, . . . cabooses in two days.: Butler.

25   Bob David purchased one of . . . stupidest thing you've ever done,": Drehs.

25   The Cockaboose Railroad has become . . . things that identifies Carolina.": Butler.

26   not until the 1912 season . . . to make a first down.: Hunter, p. 34.

26   crawling and aiding the ball . . . created the line of scrimmage: Hunter, p. 31.

26   set the length of a quarter at 15 minutes.: Hunter, p. 32.

26   "The rain plummeted . . . . concluded until nearly sundown.": Hunter, p. 32.

27   As a senior in 2006, . . . passing, and receiving in his career.: Ron Morris, "A One-Man Role Call," *The State*, Dec. 28, 2006, http://docs.newsbank.com/s/InfoWeb/aggdocs/NewsBank/11C5BC361F1EDF88, May 7, 2009.

27	In the NFL, he played cornerback, . . . played some at running back.: Morris, "A One-Man Role Call."
27	"I believe I was being . . . He has done for me,": Morris, "A One-Man Roll Call."
28	The team that time has forgotten,": Bob Spear, "Dream Team," *The State*, Feb. 9, 2005, http://docs.newsbank.com/s/InfoWeb/aggdocs/NewsBank/1082C69A2822EF32, May 6, 2009.
28	"We're the best-kept secret . . . standard for basketball excellence.": Spear, "Dream Team."
28	"Those two seasons, we ranked . . . in a battle of No. 1 and No. 2: Spear, "Dream Team."
29	In 1892, when the students of . . . they selected the Jaguars.: Simpson, *Gamecocks Handbook*, p. 7.
29	until the 1902 season, which was . . . "fought like gamecocks": Price, *Tales from the Gamecocks' Roost*, p. 2.
29	against Clemson,: Griffin, p. 15.
29	"are known for their courage . . . fight to the death.": Price, *Tales from the Gamecocks' Roost*, p. 1.
29	The nickname was actually written . . . the name to one word.: Hunter, pp. 19, 22.
29	"became unofficially official" . . . poor little gamecock.": Griffin, p. 15.
29	the players called themselves the "Carolina Chicks.": "The Basis for Today," *South Carolina 2008-09 Women's Basketball: The Gold Standard*, p. 146, http://gamecocksonline.com/cstv.com/sports/w-baskbl/spec-rel/08-09-med-guide.html, April 22, 2009.
29	Helen Timmersman, the school's first . . . plate that read "Chicks.": Price, *Tales from the Gamecocks' Roost*, p. 7.
29	the consensus arose among . . . teams became the "Lady Gamecocks,": Price, *Tales from the Gamecocks' Roost*, p. 8.
30	In the bottom of the inning, . . . if he had still been coaching.: Tom Price, *Tales from the Gamecocks' Roost*, p. 196.
31	They led 6-3 in the third quarter . . . We were ready for it,": Steve Wiseman, "Bennett's Play Picks up Gamecocks," *The State*, Oct. 3, 2004, http://docs.newsbank.com/s/InfoWeb/aggdocs/NewsBank/10583F1EE1851E89, May 6, 2009.
32	"there was absolutely nothing . . . scratched Kentucky off his list.: Scoppe and Bennett, p. 51.
32	most folks figured he was . . . see that girl again.": Scoppe and Bennett, p. 52.
33	He was "a lifelong bachelor . . . well as varsity stars." Price, *Tales from the Gamecocks' Roost*, p. 213.
33	Freeman was 27 when he . . . Among his players was Frank McGuire.: Price, *Tales from the Gamecocks' Roost*, p. 212.
33	He was an innovative coach, . . . still wanted to play.: Price, *Tales from the Gamecocks' Roost*, p. 213.
33	He lived in the Heart of Columbia . . . under the streetlights to read.: Price, *Tales from the Gamecocks' Roost*, p. 214.
33	The only technical foul . . . died eight months later,: Price, *Tales from the Gamecocks' Roost*, p. 215.
33	"one of the greatest basketball coaches of all time.": Price, *Tales from the Gamecocks' Roost*, p. 212.
34	It's a gene thing,": Michael Smith, "Passing Is in Her Genes," *The State*, Jan. 10, 2002, http://docs.newsbank.com/s/InfoWeb/aggdocs/NewsBank/0F0FAA882B7CBCDE.
34	Ciocan looked first to the . . . on the assist-to-turnover ratio.:

Smith, "Passing Is in Her Genes."

34   Her mother played ten seasons . . . centered on assists and turnovers.: Smith "Passing Is in Her Genes."

34   In Romania, she played wing . . . they knew Ciocan would find them.: Smith, "Passing Is in Her Genes."

35   was a late cut and returned . . . "I thought I was on the squad,": Bob Spear, "Addison a Star Once He Got to Play," *The State*, May 13, 2004, http://docs.newsbank.com/s/InfoWeb/aggdocs/NewsBank/10291DC2567B3F18, May 6, 2009.

35   Just before the game on Friday . . . Addison called "absolutely ridiculous,": Spear, "Addison a Star."

35   was widely considered the league's best linebacker: "Tom Addison," *Wikipedia, the free encyclopedia*, http://en.wikipedia.org.wiki/Tom_Addison, May 21, 2009.

36   Years later he said the play . . . a mistake on his part.: Tom Price, "Where Are They Now? Bobby Bryant," *South Carolina Gamecock Athletics*. Oct. 10, 2003, http://gamecocksonlive.cstv.com/sports/m-footbl/spec-rel/101003aaa.html, April 23, 2009.

36   Dietzel insisted his punt . . . into the clear around the 30,.: Price, *Tales from the Gamecocks' Roost*, p. 64.

37   I just look at myself as a golfer,": Joseph Person, "Battle Having an Impact on Minority Golfers," *The State*, May 6, 2004, http://docs.newsbank.com/s/InfoWeb/aggdocs/NewsBank/1026CF29EB96347D, May 6, 2009.

37   "the best golfer in the nation . . . and extraordinary leadership.": "Women's Golf: Erica Battle Profile," *South Carolina Gamecock Athletics*, http://gamecocksonline.cstv.com/sports/w-golf/mtt/battle_erica00.html, May 18, 2009.

37   She was also the first . . . when she was 7.: Person, "Battle Having an Impact."

37   She got tired of . . . to show him how to play.: "Erica Battle Profile."

37   When she was 15, . . . really a reality for herself.": Person, "Battle Having an Impact."

37   Life is an adventure. . . . going to happen next.: Bettinger, p. 74.

38   With 1:27 left in the third, . . . on the bottom of a huge pileup.: Bob Cole, "Atkins' Gift Helps USC to Victory," *The State*, Sept. 7, 1997, http://docs.newsbank..com/s/InfoWeb/aggdocs/NewsBank/0F0F8301563DB5E8, May 7, 2009.

38   "To be honest, that was a gift," . . . I'm not going to argue with.": Cole, "Atkins' Gift."

38   "I guess it turned out . . . we were on that play.": Cole, "Atkins' Gift."

39   "the Gamecocks apparently started thinking about [their] victory celebration.": Michael Smith, "Fantastic Finish," *The State*, Jan. 2, 2002, http://docs.newsbank.com/s/InfoWeb/aggdocs/NewsBank/0F0D07FC9CF63165, May 6, 2009.

39   Ohio State scored on the last . . . a celebratory ride around the field.": Smith, "Fantastic Finish."

40   On Feb. 1, though, against Cincinnati . . . and a prayer found the net: Price, *Tales from the Gamecocks' Roost*, p. 204.

40   It's amazing. Some of the . . . found in a Christian man.: Bettinger, p. 121.

41   DuPre (1968-70) was South Carolina's . . . only 5-5 and 150 pounds,: Price, *Tales from the Gamecocks' Roost*, p. 75.

41   DuPre had missed two earlier . . . for the longest field goal.: Simpson, *Gamecocks Handbook*, p. 59.

41   In the press box, assistant coach . . . "two very attractive young ladies.": Price, *Tales from the Gamecocks' Roost*, pp. 75-76.

42   Hold planned to walk on at Arizona State after junior college: Alex Riley, "Gamecock Greats: Mike Hold," *The Daily Gamecock*, Nov. 4, 2005, http://media.www.dailygamecock.com/media/storage/paper247/news/2005/11/04, May 2, 2009.

42	"I made two Ds and a B . . . and started making friends.": Scoppe and Bennett, p. 88.
42	"a loosey-goosey type of guy. . . . to at least do that.": Scoppe and Bennett, p. 88.
42	"was the best decision I've ever made in my life.": Scoppe and Bennett, p. 86.
43	In the spring, head coach Mark Berson . . . capable of something like this.": Bob Cole, "Midfielder Haiduk Claims Gamecocks Became Believers," *The State*, Dec. 2, 1993, http://docs.newsbank.com/s/InfoWeb/aggdocs/NewsBank/0F0F824765AE540B, May 7, 2009.
43	"Berson didn't inherit a winning tradition; he created one.": Bob Gillespie, "It's Halcyon Days for USC Soccer," *The State*, Nov. 29, 1993, http://docs.newsbank.com/s/InfoWeb/aggdocs/NewsBank/0-F0F82474D16DF89, May 7, 2009.
43	I think God made it simple. Just accept him and believe.: Bettinger, p. 47.
44	Fusci grew up in Greenwich Village in the 1930s and '40s: Scoppe and Bennett, p. 185.
44	had an appointment with a coach . . . Enright approached him,: Scoppe and Bennett, p. 186.
44	In his first game, against . . . cough up the tobacco: Scoppe and Bennett, p. 187.
45	their first "bonafide" invitation: Hunter, p. 198.
45	Dietzel's excellence as a promoter and fundraiser was on display: Hunter, p. 212.
45	Dietzel argued that because . . . for the rise in expectations.": Simpson, *Gamecocks Handbook*, p. 64.
45	"All those loyal people who . . . just thrills and moral victories.": Hunter, p. 216.
46	"I've been working 26 years . . . what Shawn has gone through.": Ron Morris, "It's Closing Time," *The State*, Feb. 12, 2006, http://docs.newsbank.com/s/InfoWeb/aggdocs/NewsBank/10FC114FCB788, May 7, 2009.
46	In October 2002, his brother . . . brother's initials in the dirt.: Morris, "It's Closing Time."
47	"Aware that football was the latest . . . hired its first football coach,: Griffin, p. 3.
47	Perhaps the domfiting news . . . the administration into action.: Griffin, p. 4.
47	the team did not leave for . . . from their oyster luncheon.": Griffin, p. 5.
47	left coaching after the season to begin his successful law practice,: Griffin, p. 6.
47	called it a "miracle" that the boys could play at all.: Griffin, p. 5.
48	A trim and fit wide receiver, . . . pulled out his driver's license;: Ray Glier, "Now Playing," *Blackfive*, http://www.blackfive.net/main/2004/09/retired_paratro.html, May 19, 2009.
48	which was not in existence when Frisby graduated from high school,: "Receiver Will Suit Up for South Carolina," *ESPNU College Football*, Sept. 23, 2004, http://sports.espn.go.com/ncf/news/story?id=1887537, May 19, 2009.
48	"He's going to play this year because he deserves to play,": "Receiver Will Suit Up."
48	"The last thing I want to be . . . and fulfill a dream.": Glier.
48	On the Saturday night following . . . he never made contact.: Steve Wiseman, "'Pops' Finally Sees Playing Time," *The State*, Sept. 26, 2004, http://docs.newsbank.com/s/InfoWeb/aggdocs/NewsBank/1055F0B43669656F, May 6, 2009.
48	fulfilling a promise Steve Spurrier made before the season began.: "Tim Frisby," *South Carolina Gamecock Athletics*, http://gamecocksonline.cstv.com/sports/m-footbl/mtt/frisby_tim00.html, May 19, 2009.
49	At a summer camp for local . . . loyal assistant than your husband.": Josh Penrod, "Husband-Wife Duo Together at Last," *The State*, Oct. 7, 2001, http://docs.newsbank.com/s/InfoWeb/aggdocs/NewsBank0EF0564E6608F9C7, May 6, 2009.
50	he grew up on a farm about six miles out in the country.: Scoppe

and Bennett, p. 9.

50   "They couldn't understand me, . . . about the first two weeks,": Scoppe and Bennett, p. 11.

50   Reeves considered himself a . . . "could throw halfway decent,": Scoppe and Bennett, p. 14.

51   The readers of The State . . . in South Carolina history.: Scoppe and Bennett, p. 49.

51   Grantz benefitted from Coach . . . Grantz was made for it.: Scoppe and Bennett, p. 44.

51   "South Carolina's offensive line . . . knew how to read it.": Scoppe and Bennett, p. 46.

51   "We just rolled that day, . . . end of a great, fun career.": Scoppe and Bennett, p. 48.

52   he was using the likes of . . . all but two of USC's points.: Price, *Tales from the Gamecocks' Roost*, p. 46.

52   When nationally ranked Duke . . . breathe on the opposing center.: Price, *Tales from the Gamecocks' Roost*, p. 48.

53   He was a good player but . . . were ahead of him.: Joseph Person, "Cornerstones: Robinson Grows into USC's Defensive Leader," *The State*, Nov. 21, 2003, http://docs.newsbank.com/s/InfoWeb/aggdocs/NewsBank/0FEFC86BB9939B77, May 6, 2009.

53   "I was wrong,": Person, "Cornerstones."

53   "He's a cool cat to . . . people can get along with.": Person, "Cornerstones."

54   He roomed with Hawkins in Columbia;: Hunter, p. 151.

54   they had played together . . . since they weren't paying me.": Hunter, p. 152.

54   "constant cohort for campus shenanigans.": Hunter, p. 151.

54   They had a 1927 Rio . . . Bodkin wasn't like other people.": Hunter, pp. 151-52.

54   Bodkin would stick a pin . . . or the pros or anywhere.": Hunter, p. 152.

55   I wanted to do what was right in my heart.": "One More Go-Round," *cnnsi.com*, Aug. 16, 2000, http://sportsillustrated.cnn.com/baseball/college/news/2008/08/16/sc_bouknight_ap, May 13, 2009.

55   "maybe the greatest season . . . ran to the Heisman Trophy.": "One More Go-Round."

55   he wrestled with it until . . . when the decision was made,": "One More Go-Round."

55   even the governor wrote Bouknight a letter thanking him for staying.: "One More Go-Round."

55   I wanted to do what . . . was right was coming back.: "One More Go-Round."

56   On Sept. 27, South Carolina . . . deflected a pass in the end zone.: Simpson, *Gamecocks Handbook*, p. 79.

57   "kind of eerie.": Neil White, "'Storybook Ending,'" *The State*, July 11, 2010, http://www.thestate.com/2010/07/11/1372586/storybook-ending.html, July 13, 2010.

57   "very much into the game . . . with pitching coach Mike Calvi," White.

57   The two coaches were standing . . . and shook his head.: White.

57   You go through times . . . something is going to happen.: White.

58   when the young English stood . . . did what I was supposed to do.": Steve Wiseman, "USC's English a Star On and Off the Court," *The State*, Sept. 14, 2008, http://www.thestate.com/gogamecocks/mensbasketball/story/523873.html, May 21, 2009.

59   Be late, be left.": Price, *Tales from the Gamecocks' Roost*, p. 172.

59   as one of his first acts as athletic director,: Price, *Tales from the Gamecocks' Roost*, p. 175.

59   in the early 1960s when the . . . the Gamecocks won the meet.: Price, *Tales from the Gamecocks' Roost*, p. 173.

60   Winn may have been the most . . . it's a little crazy sometimes,": Evan Woodbury, "Teams Embrace Superstition," *The State*, June 12, 2004, http://docs.newsbank.com/s/InfoWeb/aggdocs/NewsBank/1033419CD72472E1, May 6, 2009.

60   I'd use the same bat all year if I could.: Woodbury.

61   the crowd was settling in . . . they did the bunny hop: Griffin, p. 103.

61   "stumbled, bumbled, and fell all over each other.": Hunter, p. 175.

61   They paired off with one . . . the other milking them.: Griffin, p. 103.

61   A center snapped a ball . . . and kicked it backwards.: Hunter, p. 175.

61   Players blew kisses into . . . juice all over the place.: Griffin, p. 103.

61   "Those trusting Clemson bumpkins . . . in the history of the series.": Griffin, p. 103.

61   When you run trick plays . . . folks question your sanity.: Bettinger, p. 32.

62   She was hired by Paul Dietzel . . . special dishes for her boys.: Price, *Tales from the Gamecocks' Roost*, p. 234.

62   Jeff Grantz liked macaroni and . . . had them about twice a year.": Price, *Tales from the Gamecocks' Roost*, p. 235.

62   "only person who could overspend an unlimited budget.": Price, *Tales from the Gamecocks' Roost*, p. 234.

63   "a competitive blonde softball player . . . USC played fast-pitch softball.: Alex Riley, "USC Hall of Fame Inductees: Tiff Tootle," *The Daily Gamecock*, Sept. 13, 2006, http://media.www.dailygamecock.com/media/storage/paper247/news/2006/09/13, May 11, 2009.

63   "My dad made a video; . . . all worked out from there,": Riley, "USC Hall of Fame."

63   "It was awesome to be able to play and have that team success,": Riley, "USC Hall of Fame."

64   "My goal had been to get one interception per game,": Scoppe and Bennett, p. 162.

64   "was probably my favorite . . . out-jump the receiver.": Scoppe and Bennett, p. 163.

64   He read his Bible. . . . I sleep the entire time.": Scoppe and Bennett, p. 162.

65   When she was in elementary school . . . Now I'm cool with it.": Joseph Person, "At Home in the Paint," *The State*, Feb. 23, 2003, http://docs.newsbank.com/s/InfoWeb/aggdocs/NewsBank/0F96765D0AEF8ABZ, May 6, 2009.

65   she was never an elbow-throwing ruffian on the court,: Person, "At Home in the Paint."

66   South Carolina – both the school and the state – was desperate for a local hero,": Duncan Brantley, "16. South Carolina," *SportsIllustrated*, Sept. 4, 1985. http://vault.sportsillutrated.cnn.com/vault/article/magazine/MAG1119839/index.htm, April 27, 2009.

66   Morrison showed up for a press . . . "it was clean and it fit,": Bob Gillespie, "The Man in Black," *The State*, Feb. 8, 2009, http://www.thestate.com/gogamecocks/football/story/677895.html, April 27, 2009.

66   Starting in 1987, black became . . . for the team entrance.: "Joe Morrison," *Wikipedia, the free encyclopedi*a, http://en.wikipedia.org/wiki/Joe_Morrison, April 27, 2009.

66   "Joe Morrison did it at the . . . at him as the benchmark.": Gillespie.

67   They were arrested the Tuesday before the game,: Simpson, *Gamecocks Handbook*, p. 32.

67   Shortly before game time, . . . and the gates were closed.: Griffin, p. 76.

67	They simple rushed the gates, . . . stadium like killer bees.": Griffin, p. 77.
67	"You couldn't see anything but the playing field, and not all of that": Hunter, p. 108.
67	"I'd look around for a substitute . . . between me and my bench.": Griffin, p. 77.
67	It was almost impossible to do any coaching.": Hunter, p. 108.
67	Jimmy Byrnes, who was then . . . Carolina players on the sideline.": Griffin, p. 77.
68	During his junior year in . . . you can go a long way.": Bob Cole, "Phillips at Home at USC," *The State*, May 6, 1993, http://docs.newsbank.com/s/InfoWeb/aggdocs/NewsBank/0F0F8239EC02BC0F, May 7, 2009.
68	[Coach Switzer] was the only one . . . he'd like to see me.: Cole, "Phillips at Home at USC."
69	His father left when . . . and scored four touchdowns.: Mike Delnagro, "Rogers: Portrait of Perseverance," *Sports Illustrated*, Sept. 22, 1980, http://vault.sportsillustrated.cnn.com/vault/article/magazine/MAG1115703/index.htn, April 21, 2009.
70	Gamecock fans "danced in the aisles, . . . (and two coaches) in the making.": Bob Gillespie, "Losing Streak, Goal Posts Both Go Down," *The State*, Sept. 3, 2000, http://docs.newsbank.com/s/InfoWeb/aggdocs/NewsBank/0F0F75D1B01FA271, May 6, 2009.
70	"South Carolina had known only sorrow, frustration, disappointment.": Gillespie, "Losing Streak."
70	with 36 seconds left, . . . he played brilliantly,": Gillespie, "Losing Streak."
70	put the drought on life support.: Gillespie, "Losing Streak."
70	"This is a starting point,": Gillespie, "Losing Streak."
71	An LSU player stole the ball . . . Bownton drew a technical foul.: Steve Wiseman, "Gamecocks Hold on in Wild Finish," *The State*, Jan. 25, 2004, http://docs.newsbank.com/s/InfoWeb/aggdocs/NewsBank/10053449BcA8D2CB, May 6, 2009.
71	I got caught up in the heat of the battle.: Wiseman, "Gamecocks Hold On."
72	He endured two years of . . . driving time away in South Carolina.: Kamon Simpson, "USC's Love Has Plenty of Heart," *The State*, Oct. 2, 1997, http://docs.newsbank.com/s/InfoWeb/aggdocs/NewsBank/0EB586BAF2012812, May 7, 2009.
72	"I just made it up . . . the start at middle linebacker,": Simpson, "USC's Love."
73	In the championship game of the NCAA . . . Bass struck the batter out," Price, *Tales from the Gamecocks' Roost*, p. 139.
73	pitching on only two days' rest,: Price, *Tales from the Gamecocks' Roost*, p. 139.
73	When coach Bobby Richardson came . . . His tears wouldn't let him.: Bob Spear, "All-Time Team – After 25 Years, Bass' Place Is Solid," *The State*, June 11, 2000, http://docs.newsbank.com/s/InfoWeb/aggdocs/NewsBank/0F0F75CF5330F5D0, May 6, 2009.
74	"If I'd have known how important . . . able to take the snap,": Scoppe and Bennett, p. 99.
74	color commentator for the . . . recommended him for the job.: "Through His Many Carolina Associations, Tommy Suggs Continues to Be a Big Player," *University of South Carolina: Spotlight: Alumni*, http://www.sc.edu/spotlight/item.php?catid=3&sid=11&a=, April 21, 2009.
74	"Tom, you're eight for eight, three to them and five to us,": Scoppe and Bennett, p. 97.
74	the Gamecocks were at the 34 . . . making sure I saw it.": Scoppe and Bennett, pp. 97-98.
75	Virginia would whip South Carolina by at least fourteen points.: Simpson, *Gamecocks Handbook*, p. 38.

75   He benched his starting . . . that way into the fourth quarter.": Simpson, *Game-cocks Handbook*, p. 39.

76   national public opinion against it . . . they reinstated football at USC.: Hunter, p. 29.

77   "a time when every day was . . . the world of Carolina basketball.": Bob Spear, "McGuire Mystique," *The State*, Dec. 21, 2007, http://docs.newsbank.com/s/In-foWeb/aggdocs/NewsBank/11DB2CF1C9696898, May 7, 2009.

77   Gary Gregor was sidelined . . . demonstrated what could be.": Spear, "McGuire Mystique."

77   "We do not choose whether . . . on which we will stand.": R. Alan Culpepper, "The Gospel of Luke: Introduction, Commentary, and Reflections," *The New Interpreter's Bible*, Vol. IX (Nashville: Abingdon Press, 1998), p. 153.

78   Julius Derrick led the team . . . if it doesn't have the football.": Price, *Tales from the Gamecocks' Roost*, p. 159.

78   To defend his conservative approach . . . leaders had losing records.: Price, *Tales from the Gamecocks' Roost*, p. 160.

78   After the two-point conversion . . . field goal during Giese's tenure.: Price, *Tales from the Gamecocks' Roost*, p. 160.

78   Giese held closed practices . . . to check it out.: Price, *Tales from the Gamecocks' Roost*, p. 161.

78   They surprised an amorous . . . they could be alone.: Price, *Tales from the Game-cocks' Roost*, p. 162.

79   He didn't even rate a biography . . . Squad member who was redshirted.": Price, *Tales from the Gamecocks' Roost*, p. 119.

79   Kimrey did not play a single down in 1998 or 1999.: Price, *Tales from the Game-cocks' Roost*, p. 118.

79   South Carolina had seven . . . all against New Mexico State.: Price, *Tales from the Gamecocks' Roost*, p. 119.

79   On third and ten from the State 25, . . . national radio networks interviewed him: Price, *Tales from the Gamecocks' Roost*, p. 118.

79   Brother, that was big time.: Price, *Tales from the Gamecocks' Roost*, p. 119.

80   "a folk hero in South Carolina,": Price, *Tales from the Gamecocks' Roost*, p. 67.

80   Dietzel promised Richardson an increase in budget and improvement in facilities.: Price, *Tales from the Gamecocks' Roost*, p. 68.

80   with only part-time coaches . . . had never scheduled 35.: Price, *Tales from the Gamecocks' Roost*, p. 67.

80   in a game against Davidson in 1970, . . . 'Phooey on you.'": Price, *Tales from the Gamecocks' Roost*, pp. 68, 70.

81   "riled the Clemson faithful . . . Clemson for its poor sportsmanship.: Bob Spear, "Long Journey Comes to a HOF End," *The State*, Sept. 14, 2006, http://docs.newsbank.com/s/InfoWeb/aggdocs/NewsBank/114297DA8E04C2A8, May 7, 2009.

82   "South Carolina's athletic facilities charitably . . . "a real visionary.": Bob Spear, "Dietzel Put USC at Forefront," *The State*, July 19, 2006, http://docs.newsbank.com/s/InfoWeb/aggdocsNewsBank/112FCD32060C3BA8, May 7, 2009.

83   As always, the Clemson cadets . . . to enjoy the State Fair.: Griffin, pp. 12, 14.

83   A downtown merchant hung . . . the gloating gamecock's presence.: Griffin, p. 14.

83   Following the parade, . . . anything else resembling a weapon.: Hunter, p. 26.

83   A senior called out . . . "Make every shot count.": Griffin, p. 14.

83   Before blood could be shed, . . . hand-to-hand combat.": Hunter,

	p. 26.
83	That didn't work, . . . the two student bodies cheered.: Griffin, p. 14.
84	Kraft came to Columbia from . . . with 2.5 seconds on the clock.: Price, *Tales from the Gamecocks' Roost*, p. 205.
84	He inbounded the ball to . . . by exuberant teammates.: Price, *Tales from the Gamecocks' Roost*, p. 206.
84	Travis Kraft's foot injury . . . He then left school.: Price, *Tales from the Gamecocks' Roost*, p. 206.
85	The crowd turned eerily silent . . . to take the lead.: Bob Spear, "Block Is a Lock to Swing Momentum," *The State*, Sept. 30, 2007, http://docs.newsbank.com/s/InfoWeb/aggdocs/NewsBank/11C36DeeDA470148, May 7, 2009.
85	"Once I freed the center, . . . ricocheted through the arena.": Spear, "Block Is a Lock."
85	"We can finally say special teams won a game now,": Spear, "Block Is a Lock."
86	Women's sports were called "Co-Ed Athletics" . . . the intramural programs still offered today.": History of the Program: Humble Beginnings," *South Carolina 2008-09 Women's Basketball: The Gold Standard*, p. 146, http://gamecocksonline.cstv.com/sports/w-baskbl/spec-rel/08-09-media-guide.html, April 22, 2009.
86	In 1967, women's basketball began competing . . . took over the women's club team.: "History of the Program: The Basis for Today," *South Carolina 2008-09 Women's Basketball: The Gold Standard*, p. 146, http://gamecocksonline.cstv.com/sports/w-baskbl/spec-rel/08-09-media-guide.html, April 22, 2009.
87	Brewer grew up an Ohio . . . time of day – or a scholarship: Price, *Tales from the Gamecocks' Roost*, pp. 107-08.
87	Brewer had played tailback in high school . . . 14 times during the 2000 season.: Price, *Tales from the Gamecocks' Roost*, p. 107.
87	"I never dreamed anything like this would happen,": "Getting a Little Payback," *cnn/Sports Illustrated*, Jan. 2, 2001, http://sportsillustrated.cnn.com/football/college/2000/bowls/news/2001/01/01/outback_ga, April 23, 2009.
87	You're not here to prove . . . to help your teammates.: "Getting a Little Payback."
88	So he told his runners, . . . waited 27 years for this.": "2002 NCAA Women's Outdoor National Champions," *2009 South Carolina Track & Field*, p. 82, http://www.gamecocksonline.cstv.com/photos/schools/scar/sports/c-track/auto_pdf/09-trk-mg-sec-6.pdf, June 3, 2009.
89	When asked in 1995 how he . . . "That crazy Yankee quarterback.": Simpson, *Gamecocks Handbook*, p. 121.
89	Taneyhill's hair hung . . . like a mud flap.": Sally Jenkins, "Steve Taneyhill," *Sports Illustrated*, Aug. 30, 1993, http://vault.sportsillustrated.cnn.com/vault/article/magazine/MAG1138026/1/index.htm, April 21, 2009.
89	Taneyhill was jogging downfield . . . I still hear about it today.": Scoppe and Bennett, pp. 32-33.
89	signing his name on the dotted paw.: Simpson, *Gamecocks Handbook*, p. 118.
90	"the one man the Gamecocks could absolutely not do without": Doug Jolley, "Tre Kelley: 'God Answered My Prayers,'"*GamecockAnthem.com*, Jan. 8, 2007, http://southcarolina.scout.com/2/607632.html, May 11, 2009.
90	"I told the trainers, . . . a stronger and better person.": Jolley.
90	"My knee feels great," . . . working on him. It's amazing,": Jolley.
90	God definitely answered my prayers and enabled me to come back and play.: Jolley.

GAMECOCKS

BIBLIOGRAPHY

"2002 NCAA Women's Outdoor National Champions." *2009 South Carolina Track & Field*. 82. http://www.gamecocksonline.cstv.com/photos/schools/scar/sports/c-track/auto_pdf/09-trk-mg-sec-6.pdf.

Aiken, Ron. "Athletes of the Past 20 Years: Duce Staley." *The State*. 20 Sept. 2001. http://docs.newsbank.com/s/InfoWeb/aggdocs/NewsBank/0EEABC40C759A4C3.

"The Basis for Today." *South Carolina 2008-09 Women's Basketball: The Gold Standard*. 146-47. http://gamecocksonline.cstv.com/sports/w-baskbl/spec-rel/08-09-media-guide.html.

Bettinger, Jim & Julie S. *The Book of Bowden*. Nashville, TN: TowleHouse Publishing, 2001.

Brantley, Duncan. "16. South Carolina." *Sports Illustrated*. 4 Sept. 1985. http://vault.sportsillustrated.cnn.com/vault/article/magazine/MAG1119839/index.htm.

Butler, Pat. "Visionary Inventor Robinson Dies at 50: Cockaboose Inventor Changed How USC Fans Worshipped Team." *The State*. 13 April 1998. http://docs.newsbank.com/s/InfoWeb/aggdocs/NewsBank/0EB587251CE41146.

Cole, Bob. "Atkins' Gift Helps USC to Victory." *The State*. 7 Sept. 1997. http://docs.newsbank.com/s/InfoWeb/aggdocs/NewsBank/0F0F8301563DB5E8.

---. "Midfielder Haiduk Claims Gamecocks Became Believers." *The State*. 2 Dec. 1993. http://docs.newsbank.com/s/InfoWeb/aggdocs/Newsbank/0F0F824765AE540B.

---. "Phillips at Home at USC – Gamecock Coach Key in Landing Swimmer." *The State*. 6 May 1993. http://docs.newsbank.com/s/InfoWeb/aggdocs/NewsBank/0F08239EC02BC0F.

Crouch, Gail. "Legendary John Roche Returns to Columbia." *Moore School of Business Alumni News*. 26 July 2007. http://mooreschool.sc.edu/moore/pr/news/Alumni News/roche_john_returns.html.

Culpepper, R. Alan. "The Gospel of Luke: Introduction, Commentary, and Reflections." *The New Interpreter's Bible*. IX. Nashville: Abingdon Press, 1998. 1-490.

Delnagro, Mike. "Rogers: Portrait of Perseverance." *Sports Illustrated*. 22 Sept. 1980. http://vault.sportsillustrated.cnn.com/vault/article/magazine/MAG1115703/index.htm.

Drehs, Wayne. "All Aboard! Gamecocks Tailgate in Style." *ESPN.com*. 16 Oct. 2003. http://sports.espn.go.com/espn/print?id=1639333&type=page2Story.

Garber, Greg. "At What Price Olympic Glory," *ESPN.com*. 15 July 2004.

"Getting a Little Payback." *cnn/sports illustrated*. 2 Jan. 2001. http://sportsillustrated.cnn.com/football/college/2000/bowls/news/2001/01/01/outback_ga.

Gillespie, Bob. "Beating the Clock – Top Five Buzzer-Beaters in USC Men's History." *The State*. 9 Jan. 2001. http://docs.newsbank.com/s/InfoWeb/aggdocs/News Bank/0F0F75D58B693A40.

---. "It's Halcyon Days for USC Soccer." The State. 29 Nov. 1993. http://docs.newsbank.com/s/InfoWeb/aggdocs/NewsBank/0-F0F82474D16DF89.

---. "Losing Streak, Goal Posts Both Go Down." *The State*. 3 Sept. 2000. http://docs.newsbank.com/s/InfoWeb/aggdocs/NewsBank/0F0F75D1B01FA271.

---. "The Man in Black: Morrison's Legacy at USC Looms 20 Years After Death." *The State*. 8 Feb. 2009. http://www.thestate.com/gogamecocks/football/story/677895.html.

Glier, Ray. "Now Playing: The Old Man and the Football Team." *Blackfive*. http://www.blackfive.net/main/2004/09/retired_paratro.html.

193

Griffin, John Chandler. *The First Hundred Years: A History of South Carolina Football.* Atlanta: Longstreet Press, 1992.

"History of the Program." *South Carolina 2008-09 Women's Basketball: The Gold Standard.* 146-48. http://gamecocksonline.cstv.com/sports/w-baskbl/spec-rel/08-09-media-guide.html.

Hunter, Jim. *The Gamecocks: South Carolina Football.* Huntsville, AL: The Strode Publishers, 1975.

Jenkins, Sally. "Steve Taneyhill." *Sports Illustrated.* 30 Aug. 1993. http://vault.sports illustrated.cnn.com/vault/article/magazine/MAG1138026/1/index.htm.

"Joe Morrison." *Wikipedia, the free encyclopedia.* http://en.wikipedia.org/wiki/Joe_Morrison.

Jolley, Doug. "Tre Kelley: 'God Answered My Prayers.'" *GamecockAnthem.com.* 8 Jan. 2007. http://southcarolina.scout.com/2/607632.html.

Kirkpatrick, Curry. "The Toughest Kid on Anybody's Block." *Sports Illustrated.* 4 Jan. 1971. http://vault.sportsillustrated.cnn.com/vault/article/magazine/MAG1084442/index.htm.

Morris, Ron. "Berson Happy to Be USC's One and Only." *The State.* 30 Sept. 2005. http://docs.newsbank.com/s/InfoWeb/aggdocs/NewsBank/10CF8F2A418D00D0.

---. "Brawl Seals 'Momma's Boy' Label." *The State.* 22 Feb. 2008. http://docs.newsbank.com/s/InfoWeb/aggdocs/NewsBank/11F23F5A73B10C28.

---. "Forget the Ending, This Season Was a Success." *The State.* 1 Jan. 2006. http://docs.newsbank.com/s/InfoWeb/aggdocs/NewsBank/10EE396E0DC033E0.

---. "It's Closing Time." *The State.* 12 Feb. 2006. http://docs.newsbank.com/s/InfoWeb/aggdocs/NewsBank/10FC114FC22CB788.

---. "A One-Man Roll Call: Newton Will Bow Out as Most Versatile Player in USC Player." *The State.* 28 Dec. 2006. http://docs.newsbank.com/s/InfoWeb/aggdocs/NewsBank/11C5BC361F1EDF88.

---. "Steve Wadiak: The Heartbreak Kid." GoGamecocks.com. 2 Nov. 2008. http://www.thestate.com/gogamecocks/ronmorris/story/574995.html.

---. "USC Softball: Players Learn Value of Hard Work from Their Old-School Coach." *The State.* 25 May 2007. http://docs.newsbank.com/s/InfoWeb/aggdocs/NewsBank/1196EF4FA967AF88.

"One More Go-Round: Bouknight Will Be Back for Gamecocks." *cnnsi.com.* 16 Aug. 2000. http://sportsillustrated.cnn.com/baseball/college/news/2008/08/16/sc_bouknight_ap.

Penrod, Josh. "Husband-Wife Duo Together at Last." *The State.* 7 Oct. 2001. http://docs.newsbank.com/s/InfoWeb/aggdocs/NewsBank/0EF0564E6608F9C7.

Person, Joseph. "At Home in the Paint." *The State.* 23 Feb. 2003. http://docs.newsbank.com/s/InfoWeb/aggdocs/NewsBank/0F96765D0AEF8AB7.

---. "Battle Having an Impact on Minority Golfers." *The State.* 6 May 2004. http://docs.newsbank.com/s/InfoWeb/aggdocs/NewsBank/1026CF29EB96347D.

---. "Cornerstones: Robinson Grows into USC's Defensive Leader." *The State.* 21 Nov. 2003. http://docs.newsbank.com/s/InfoWeb/aggdocs/NewsBank/0FEFC86BB9939B77.

---. "Moving on Up: Now the Senior Has Become a Significant Contributor." *The State.* 22 Dec. 2007. http://docs.newsbank.com/s/InfoWeb/aggdocs/NewsBank/11E466F216592160.

---. "Road Trip: Liberty Bowl Trophy Takes a Long Hike Home to USC." *The State.* 6 Jan. 2007. http://docs.newsbank.com/s/InfoWeb/aggdocs/NewsBank/1168D4

194

A68E823008, May 7, 2009.

---. "Still on Track: USC's Natasha Hastings Thought About Quitting, Now She Is Among the Nation's Best." *The State*. 6 June 2007. http://docs.newsbank.com/s/InfoWeb/aggdocs/NewsBank/1199E6E0D401F2C0.

Price, Tom. *Tales from the Gamecocks' Roost: A Collection of the Greatest Gamecocks' Stories Ever Told*. Champaign, IL: Sports Publishing, L.L.C., 2002.

---. "Where Are they Now: Bobby Bryant." *South Carolina Gamecock Athletics*. 10 Oct. 2003. http://gamecocksonline.cstv.com/sports/m-footbl/spec-rel/101003aaa.html.

"Receiver Will Suit Up for South Carolina." *ESPNU: College Football*. http://sports.espn.go.com/ncf/news/story?id=1887537.

Riley, Alex. "Gamecock Greats: Mike Hold." *The Daily Gamecock*. 4 Nov. 2005. http://media.www.dailygamecock.com/media/storage/paper247/news/2005/11/04.

---. "USC Hall of Fame Inductees: Tiff Tootle." *The Daily Gamecock*. 13 Sept. 2006. http://media.www.dailygamecock.com/media/storage/paper247/news/2006/09/13.

Scoppe, Rick and Charlie Bennett. *Game of My Life: South Carolina: Memorable Stories of Gamecocks Football*. Champaign, IL: Sports Publishing L.L.C., 2007.

Simpson, Kamon. *Gamecocks Handbook: Stories, Stats and Stuff about South Carolina Football*. Wichita, KS: The Wichita Eagle and Beacon Publishing Co., 1996.

---. "USC"s Love Has Plenty of Heart." *The State*. 2 Oct. 1997. http://docs.newsbank.com/InfoWeb/aggdocs/NewsBank/0EB586BAF2012812.

Smith, Michael. "Fantastic Finish – Seniors Leave Legacy of School-Best 17 Wins in Two Seasons." *The State*. 2 Jan. 2002. http://docs.newsbank.com/s/InfoWeb/aggdocs/NewsBank/0F0D07FC9CF63165.

---. "Passing Is in Her Genes." *The State*. 10 Jan. 2002. http://docs.newsbank.com/s/InfoWeb/aggdocs/NewsBank/0F0FAA882B7CBCDE.

Spear, Bob. "Addison a Star Once He Got to Play." *The State*. 13 May 2004. http://docs.newsbank.com/s/InfoWeb/aggdocs/NewsBank/10291DC2567B3F18.

---. "All-Time Team – After 25 Years, Bass' Place Is Solid." *The State*. 11 June 2000. http://docs.newsbank.com/s/InfoWeb/aggdocs/NewsBank/0F0F75CF5330F5.

---. "Block Is a Lock to Swing Momentum." *The State*. 30 Sept. 2007. http://docs.newsbank.com/s/InfoWeb/aggdocs/NewsBank/11C36DEEDA470148.

---. "Dietzel Put USC at Forefront." *The State*. 19 July 2006. http://doscs.newsbank.com/s/InfoWeb/aggdocs/NewsBank/112FCD32060C3BA8.

---. "Dream Team: 94-Year-Old Alum Calls 1933-34 Hoops Squads UCS's 'Best-Kept Secret.'" *The State*. 9 Feb. 2005. http://docs.newsbank.com/s/InfoWeb/aggdocs/NewsBank/1082C69A2822EF32.

---. "Humble in the Wake of Greatness." *The State*. 1 Feb. 2003. http://docs.newsbank.com/InfoWeb/aggdocs/NewsBank/0F8F359206F6E7D7.

---. "Long Journey Comes to a HOF End." *The State*. 14 Sept. 2006. http://docs.newsbank.com/s/InfoWeb/aggdocs/NewsBank/114297DA8E04C2A8.

---. "McGuire Mystique: The Birth of the Frank McGuire Era." *The State*. 21 Dec. 2007. http://docs.newsbank.com/s/InfoWeb/aggdocs/NewsBank/11DB2CF1C969898.

---. "A Star Once He Got to Play." *The State*. 13 May 2004. http://docs.newsbank.com/s/InfoWeb/aggdocs/NewsBank/10291DC2567B3F18.

"Through His Many Carolina Associations, Tommy Suggs Continues to Be a Big Player." *University of South Carolina: Spotlight: Alumni*. http://www.sc.edu/spotlight/item/php?catid=3&sid=11&a=.

"Tim Frisby." *South Carolina Gamecock Athletics.* http://gamecocksonline.cstv.com/sports/m-footbl/mtt/frisby_tim00.html.

"Tom Addision." *Wikipedia, the free encyclopedia.* http://en.wikipedia.org/wiki/Tom_Addison.

White, Neil. "'Storybook Ending': USC's Coach Answers Questions about the Title Run, the Team's Future." *The State.* 11 July 2010. http://www.thestate.com.2010/07/11/1372586/storybook-ending.html.

Wiseman, Steve. "Bennett's Play Picks up Gamecocks." *The State.* 3 Oct. 2004. http://docs.newsbank.com/s/InfoWeb/aggdocs/NewsBank/10583F1EE1851E89.

---. "Better Times." *The State.* 30 May 2003. http://docs.newsbank.com/s/InfoWeb/aggdocs/NewsBank/0FB61689FA794D8D.

---. "Gamecocks Hold on in Wild Finish." *The State.* 25 Jan. 2004. http://docs.newsbank.com/s/InfoWeb/aggdocs/NewsBank/10053449B3A8D2CB.

---. "'Pops' Finally Sees Playing Time." *The State.* 26 Sept. 2004. http://docs.newsbank.com/s/InfoWeb/aggdocs/NewsBank/1055F0B43669656F.

---. "USC's English a Star On and Off the Court." The State. 14 Sept. 2008. http://www.thestate.com/gogamecocks/mensbasketball/story/523873.html.

"Women's Golf: Erica Battle Profile." South Carolina Gamecock Athletics. http://gamecocksonline.cstv.com/sports/w-folf/mtt/battle_erica00.html.

Woodbury, Evan. "Teams Embrace Superstition." *The State.* 12 June 2004. http://docs.newsbank.com/s/InfoWeb/aggdocs/NewsBank/1034419CD72472E1.

GAMECOCKS

INDEX
(LAST NAME, DEVOTION DAY NUMBER)

SOUTH CAROLINA

Abe 30
Lewis, Quinton 8
Locke, Bobby 85
Lombardi, Vince 24, 46, 59, 84
Love, Mark 72
Major, Chris 22
Mantle, Mickey 80
Martz, Randy 9, 30
McGee, Mike 25, 49
McGuire, Frank 3, 28, 33, 77
McIntee, Willie 8
McKie, B.J. 40
McKinley, Kenny 85
McKissick, Rion 83
McLaurin, C.H. 47
McLean, Chuck 30
Melillo, Kevin 60
Melton, Dick 59
Michaels, Al 3
Mitchell, Allen 42
Mitchell, Blake 27
Mitchell, Jimmy 74
Moore, Blake 30
Moore, John 62, 82
Morgan, Scott 5
Morris, Otis 22
Morrison, Joe 8, 16, 42, 66
Muir, Warren 2, 41
Newton, Syvelle 27, 31
Nies, Billy 59
Nix, Tyrone 27
Noe, Chuck 52
Norwood, Eric 85
Odom, Dave 12, 71, 90
Offing, Andre 70
Offord, Willie 70
Owens, Tom 3, 12
Paige, Satchel 48
Parone, Harry 18
Perlotte, Robert 56
Petty, Phil 4, 39, 70, 79

Phillips, Dan 68
Pinckney, Cleveland 79
Pinnock, Andrew 39
Posnanski, Jamie 43
Powell, Carlos 71
Price, Tom 82
Purvis, Don 41
Raines, June 9, 30
Reeves, Dan 16, 50
Reid, Mike 47
Reynolds, Kenny 62
Ribbock, John 12
Rich, Carey 3
Richardson, Bobby 73, 80
Robinson, Dunta 53
Robinson, Ed 25
Roche, John 3, 12
Rockne, Knute 78, 81
Rodgers, Bill 39
Rogers, George 16, 23, 55, 56, 62, 69
Ross, Tiffany 88
Rowland, John 28
Royal, Darrell 31
Russell, Bill 49
Sadler, Frank 42
Schroeder, John 52
Scott, Brad 20, 72
Seawright, James 66
Sharpe, Sterling 27, 66
Shea, Walt 75
Simpson, Ko 31
Smelley, Chris 85
Smith, Buck 28
Smith, Jamie 49
Smith, Shelley 49
Sossamon, Lou 44
Spurrier, Steve 7, 27, 48, 85
Staley, Duce 20
Standard, Frank 77
Strickland, Bishop 23
Suggs, Tommy 2, 41, 74

Sutton, Don 10
Swink, Marion 16
Switzer, Keith 68
Taneyhill, Steve 11, 89
Tanner, Ray 21, 46, 57
Thomas, Frank 83
Thompson, Jack 77
Timmermans, Helen 29
Tompkins, Bennie 28
Tompkins, Freddie 28
Tootle, Tiff 63
Trafford, Rodney 4
Tyler, Tremaine 31
Ujhelyi, Petra 65
Valdes-Fauli, Shawn 46
Van Bever, Mark 30
Vendt, Erik 15
Wadiak, Steve 16, 23
Wallace, Grady 24
Walvius, Susan 17, 34
Washburn, Jim 22
Washington, Demetria 88
Watson, Derek 70, 87
Watson, Melvin 40
Weaver, Daniel 39
Weaver, Earl 53
Whaley, W.H. 16, 47
White, Reggie 54, 89
Wilburn, J.R. 81
Wilkes, Del 66
Williams, Clarence 51
Wilson, Mookie 30
Winn, Brendan 60
Winters, Brian 3
Witt, Gene 75
Wooden, John 1, 14, 27, 72, 74
Woods, Sparky 89
Wright, Johnnie 56
Wuerffel, Danny 77
Zaharias, Babe 51
Zeigler, Fred 2, 41